T0129285

YOUR THIRD STORY

Author The Life You Were Meant To Live

FLIP FLIPPEN & DR. CHRIS J WHITE

iUniverse®

YOUR THIRD STORY
AUTHOR THE LIFE YOU WERE MEANT TO LIVE

iUniverse books may be ordered through booksellers or by contacting:

iUniverse
1663 Liberty Drive
Bloomington, IN 47403
www.iuniverse.com
1-800-Authors (1-800-288-4677)

ISBN: 978-1-5320-7801-9 (sc)
ISBN: 978-1-5320-7804-0 (e)

Library of Congress Control Number: 2019909026

Print information available on the last page.

iUniverse rev. date: 07/19/2019

CONTENTS

To Susan and Jennifer

ACKNOWLEDGEMENTS

Everyone who has "written on" us is a part of this book, so we want to offer a broad "we couldn't have done it without you" to those who wrote valuable things on us. To those who wrote imperfectly on us, we thank you too. You made us stronger and you are in good company because we are imperfect writers, ourselves.

We want to give a special thank you to some of the individuals who not only wrote "on" our lives but also, literally, wrote on this book. The amazing collection of talent that is The Flippen Group, in focus groups and individual conversations, helped identify weaknesses and insist on clarity. Foremost among them were Joy Chmelar, Karen Gorski, Sean Murphy, Kate Cirillo, Michael Cody, Leah Sequeira, Meredith King, and Julie Gorski.

Our primary editors—Craig Bird, Joe Terrell, and Margie Lightsey—played a huge role in the art of communication and in making the content come alive.

The production and promotion team, Susan Flippen and Tanya Peterson, helped make sure this book wasn't just read by our friends and family.

Finally, as men who gratefully acknowledge the gift of incredible wives and great families, we express from the depths of our souls and hearts appreciation to Susan Flippen and Jennifer White for being the greatest writers we ever could have wanted and needed. Our lives, our children, our homes, and these pages are filled with your love and sacrifice.

CHAPTER 1

INTRODUCTION: THE BACK STORY

"The only person you are destined to become is the person you decide to be."
　　　　　　　　　　　- Ralph Waldo Emerson

This book is personal for me. More personal, perhaps, than I have ever admitted to myself or anyone else. As I write this, I am sitting in New York for meetings with several top business people in the financial world. And next week I head to Africa to work on a conservation program relocating giraffes, rhinos, and lions.

It's fun to celebrate a life filled with joy and fulfillment. But for me, there have also been dark and dismal times.

It was almost 5:00 p.m. on December 24 many years ago; a stormy day of sleet and rain—that miserable "in between" weather a Texas winter can produce at a moment's notice.

My young son, Micah, and I were finishing some Christmas shopping, and I swung by my office to meet briefly with a few of my board members before the year came to an end.

In the non-profit world, the organization I had founded 16 years prior was highly respected and successful. It was one of the few free outpatient mental health clinics in the South. Our large clinical staff cared for hundreds of patients each month. We also ran high adventure programs for kids from across all spectrums of life, as well as clinical training programs for up-and-coming therapists. I loved every minute of it.

It's hard to describe the immense satisfaction I felt whenever I looked at the team I had enlisted to join arms with me in making a real difference.

Those feelings stopped on that day in December.

Three of my board members abruptly informed me I was being terminated, effective immediately. Your mind does such interesting things in such moments.

Why? What in the world is happening? I appointed you to the board—can you even do this?

In the midst of my shock, I asked if this was a joke. It wasn't.

They offered no explanation other than that they had agreed to never discuss it with anyone, including spouses and me. No reason, nothing other than a small severance and a request that they be allowed to "host a party to celebrate all you have done for the community as you go on to what you will do next."

Stunned, I asked, "Am I supposed to go to a party when I don't even know what is happening?" Silently I wondered, *How can I do that? Am I expected to be duplicitous about all of this?*

Then they insisted, "Please agree not to discuss what is happening, as we don't want to hurt our organization." All I could think was, *It's not your organization. You didn't build it. Why would I ever hurt the company I built? Is this really happening?*

The meeting lasted about five minutes. My life changed forever.

I walked out of what had been my office and said goodbye to my secretary—Barbara Knowles—and took Micah to finish his Christmas shopping. I didn't tell either of them what had just transpired.

We got home as night fell and I donned my bad weather gear for a much-needed walk down the country road where we lived. Eventually, I crawled through a fence, went deeper into the woods, sat down against a huge oak tree in a sleet storm—and wept.

I cried until I could catch my breath and then quietly sobbed as the questions flooded over me: *What will I do? How will we live? Can I take care of my family? What will people think of me? What's next?*

Then I cried some more.

As lightning flashed, I saw a large tree across an open area. I noticed it was dying because a pipeline easement had been cut too close to it. The thought of that old tree dying unleashed another huge wave of sadness and more tears. *Dear God, why is this happening? I don't understand. What have I done?*

Then I realized something I knew deep within me. That tree was a victim; it had been killed by something over which it had no control. That tree was a victim, but I was not!

I still had more days to come and I had children that needed me. I had choices and I had things no one could take away from me. I had my character, my integrity, my experiences, my life, my children, my abilities, and my friends.

One dear friend, David Shellenberger, was a great help through it all, literally giving me the clothes off his back. We need each other, don't we? Life is tough when we face it alone, so why face it alone? There are others who walk the same path, so let's walk it with courage and hope and forgiveness.

Days later, a front-page article gushed about the organization and all we had accomplished. It said I was leaving with great plans for the future (unknown to me, of course). It was a kind article and scores of people congratulated me on my future. I felt conflicted.

A few months after my termination, Barbara joined me as executive assistant in my counseling practice and several months after that, the board learned they had made a mistake based on incorrect information. I still had to rebuild my life, but I have no regrets nor any bitterness toward them. It took a while, but I laid those thoughts down. It's difficult to walk into the future with a heavy load on your back.

Today, I own the land and the ranch where I sat and cried. We have built nine companies so far, with more to come. I would never have been *here* without being *there*. That is something you must understand: there is no *here* without a *there*!

That is what this book is about. The marvelous truth is that there is *more*. There is always more, and I want you to know about it and how to find it. And it's not about money or power or possessions.

It's about life! The biggest, best, happiest, fullest life you could ever imagine.

I have been broken before and perhaps will be again. I have been terribly sad and felt beyond despair. I know what it is to want to give up, to be unable to sleep, to lose weight (when you don't want to), to cry yourself to sleep, to hold it all in so that others don't worry about what is happening.

And I know that even as I write these things there will be those who read it and wonder, "So who is he and what *really* happened?" Well, that is also a fear many people face and it keeps them stuck in a story they can't get out of. I don't live in that story or those fears, and I don't want others to either.

If it were not for that tragic and unjust time in my life and that desperate sense of loss, I would not be here. So much pain, but I am thankful.

Through days such as those, you come to know who your friends really are. More importantly, you come to know who *you* really are. It takes guts to face life, and it takes courage to share your dark moments and struggles.

To those of you who have gone through hard trials and are writing a great story, congratulations! For those of you who have not started that new story, exciting times are ahead, my friend.

There is more for you—much, much more than you ever dreamed.

CHAPTER 2

YOUR FIRST STORY: THE ONE GIVEN TO YOU

"Maybe there is more to your story."

\- Unknown

A STORY IS DELIVERED

I'll never forget waiting for our first grandchild to arrive.

We lived in the same town as my son Matthew and daughter-in-law Heather, so we had nine months together to feed our excitement. At every opportunity, I would pat Heather's belly and whisper sweet words of joy and encouragement to my granddaughter. And like most expectant mothers, she endured the patting knowing we were all celebrating a great joy.

For medical reasons, the doctors advised that a Cesarean

delivery (C-section) would be necessary. You know what's great about a C-section? You get to schedule it! That means grandparents get to skip all the stressful waiting and just show up for the grand finale!

On the appointed day, there wasn't an empty chair in the waiting room. Never before or since have I seen a birth where so many family members and friends were on standby.

By the time the nurses navigated the overcrowded hallways and wheeled Heather into surgery, her "operating room" hair and makeup were pretty much history. She had been kissed on, cried over and hugged by so many people who loved her!

Matthew, covered in a delivery room gown, excitedly followed her through the swinging doors. After what seemed like only a few minutes, he was holding our beautiful new granddaughter, Jessica, in his arms.

And just like that, an incredible new light source appeared in my emotional heaven.

SAME BIRTHDAY, DIFFERENT ENVIRONMENTS

As we eagerly waited for Jessica's grand entry, another expectant mother—who looked no more than 17—was wheeled down the same hallway.

I noticed that no one hovered with anticipation in the waiting room or trailed alongside to support and love on her. No father or mother. No spouse or friend. No sister or brother. No aunts, uncles or cousins. Just two nurses, pushing her hospital bed down the long, sterile hallway.

I will never forget my feelings as the delivery room doors swung shut. She looked anxious and worried, and several of us offered encouraging words and best wishes as she made her way by.

Later, in the hallway where visitors admire newborns while huddled around the wired glass windows, the two babies lay side by side. Equally beautiful and equally loved by their mothers, sharing the same nurses and breathing the same air. I stood with tears of love for my granddaughter and a sense of sadness for the other baby.

The next morning, we helped Matthew and Heather bring Jessica home. As we loaded them into the car, I watched the other young mom get into a cab with her beautiful little girl, just the two of them.

As I write this, I still wonder what became of that other baby. It's possible she was also loved by many others and has had a good life. I hope she is feeling cherished by people who think of her every day, as we do our Jessica.

That is my hope.

As precious as Jessica's story is to us, there is one thing we have to remember: she didn't write that story.

She lived it. We wrote it.

SOMETHING DOES COME FROM NOTHING

Many psychologists believe we enter life with an emotional and intellectual *tabula rasa*—Latin for "blank slate"—that becomes filled with knowledge over time as our senses feed it impressions and information.

You don't have to read Latin or study child development to be written on. In fact, you don't really have a say in the matter. Before we can assemble coherent thoughts or feelings, our blank slate is filled with notes.

I was scribbled on as a child, much more harshly than you might guess. After all, my biography says my first book, *The Flip Side* (also co-authored by Chris), was a *New York Times* best seller, and my wife Susan and I were chosen by Ernst and Young as Entrepreneurs of the Year. I've had the senior role in building several companies, and I started a 500-acre nonprofit residential treatment center for at-risk kids. Life has been good—in most ways.

But here's what is never included in my press release biography: my birth was the result of an affair. I barely scraped by with a high school diploma, fourth from the bottom of my class. And no, there weren't five in my senior class! (Trust me, I was counting!) I was eight the first time my dad beat me until I was unconscious, and 21 the last time.

I have a learning disability with a terrible name—dyscalculia—so multiplication tables are pretty much unknown territory for me. A few years ago, a third grader approached me after I confessed this fact at one of my speaking engagements and tried to reassure me that I "probably" knew the fives! Yes, I at least had those memorized.

That comforting comment was quickly followed up by another classmate patting me on the arm while saying, "Mr. Flip, you have to know the ones, too…and the zeros!" She was right—I do know those—so as I smiled and instantly felt better, she seemed glad to have boosted my spirits. I should have offered her a job on our accounting team—she probably knew more about my financial spreadsheets than I did!

When the teacher announced that if I were in their class, they would help me with math, the group cheered. That was good writing on me.

Different people and events give us roles to play and scripts to read. People wrote on me that I was not smart or lovable or worthy of affection, just an easily distracted kid who didn't pay attention.

One member of my family was in high school when a friend

of hers commented that her toes looked fat. What does that even mean, and what kind of friend would say that? But once the script was handed to her and she read it, she refused to wear sandals for the next three years.

Once they are written, we start reading the scripts and playing the roles given to us—often without a second thought. I accepted all the things written about me as if they were true. Like all children, I was young, and these were the big people in my life, so what they said had to be true.

INFORMATION RECEIVED BEFORE BIRTH

Not only is the fact that we don't write our First Story a super-sized problem, it is also long-lived. The earliest notations on our First Story precede the date on our birth certificate. We don't get to choose where we are born, the homes we grow up in, where we attend school, who our parents are, or a hundred other variables in our early life.

Only a few weeks after conception, the fetus begins producing neurons in the brain to interpret the signals a baby is hearing and feeling. Touch receptors start forming around the eighth week. Toward the end of the second trimester, the fetal nervous system is so developed that a baby is startled by loud noises, and several weeks before birth, a baby can be calmed by the mother's voice.

Before drawing our first breath, our brain connects physical sensations and emotional feelings with specific pain or pleasure. We don't ask for all this information. It is simply supplied to us. It then shapes who we are, or at least who we think we are. All we do is absorb everything that happens around us or to us.

At birth, a baby can hear, smell, taste and is highly sensitive to touch. We pick up and record more signals, whether good or bad. Neurons pick up actions and expressions and sounds, whether a frown, a laugh, a frustration, a shout, or a smile. Each signal gets internalized and even if we interpret incorrectly, we still attach meaning to it. In other words, long before we know our ABCs, we learn how to read.

THE AUTHORITY FIGURE FACTOR

As we grow up, we stay especially tuned to messages from authority figures, those people whose love and approval we desire. These early messages from people important to us prove quite sticky in our First Story—they are hard to dislodge. Thus, a child who is told they are lazy or stupid will internalize that message and often live down to that classification. And of course positive messages from authority figures can be just as important and enduring.

Which authority figures impact us the most? Early on, it's the people who raise us.

There is plenty of research on early-stage parental influence, but for this conversation two truths are highly relevant. First, even though authority figures have the strongest voice, they aren't necessarily the healthiest. Many people carry a significant amount of baggage into their relationships with us.

Second, whoever wants or needs the relationship the least has the most power. This point is important to understand, as it applies to so many areas—negotiations, hiring and firing decisions, dating relationships and marriages—virtually every area of our lives. This is a sobering concept in determining where you stand with someone. But it's an especially scary reality for children raised by dysfunctional adults. It reminds me of a t-shirt I saw that stated, "I put the fun in dysfunctional!" Funny t-shirt, but not a funny environment in which to raise a child. The person who cares the least usually has the most power and therefore, the ability to do the most damage.

This is not to say there can't be pushback against an authority figure's potential negative impact in your life, but it is especially difficult to overcome those messages.

In adolescence, authority figures and people important to us continue to grab pens and write upon our lives—they may be parents, grandparents, teachers, coaches, band directors, youth leaders, dance instructors, friends, or siblings. We are surrounded by people who want us to follow the scripts they write. Many of those people hold distortions of their own First Stories that they unwittingly impress upon us.

This is the uncomfortable reality of our First Story. Other people write the story, and we live it out. The story could be good or bad. The odds are high it's a little bit of both.

Know this: Your First Story is part of your life, but *you didn't write it*. Your First Story is not your true story.

Recap of Key Points:

- You didn't write your First Story.
- A lot is written on us before birth.
- At birth, we pick up on expressions, reactions, and body language.
- Authority figures in particular have a powerful influence on our First Story.
- Your First Story shouldn't be your final story.

Reflection/Discussion Questions:

- Which item in the "Recap of Key Points" jumps out at you the most?
- Who are the top two or three people who wrote on you the earliest?
- Into what type of environment were you born?

CHAPTER 3

YOUR SECOND STORY: THE ONE YOU TELL YOURSELF

> *"Who are we but the stories we tell ourselves, about ourselves, and believe?"*
>
> - Scott Turow, *Ordinary Heroes*

THE ORIGIN OF YOUR SECOND STORY

As we experience our First Story, we begin the story we tell ourselves—our Second Story—because we don't know any better. The lines between our First Story and Second Story are blurry because our Second Story isn't written on blank sheets of paper. Rather, it consists of mental notes in the margins of our minds and over the erasures of our First Story.

Our Second Story consists of edited and remixed parts of

our First Story, a collection of impressions and beliefs we can draw upon as needed for particular situations. Second Stories are slippery little suckers because we pretend—and mostly believe—we have complete editorial oversight over our internal script. And the stories let us think that way and reinforce themselves, even the ones we are plagiarizing from others.

The story usually defaults one of three ways: we overvalue ourselves, undervalue ourselves, or do a little bit of both.

And then we fight to maintain the charade.

BETTER THAN AVERAGE EFFECT

Psychologists refer to the overvaluing option as the Better Than Average Effect (BTAE). Extensive research by Nicholas Epley and David Dunning of Cornell University found that "people typically believe they are more likely to engage in selfless, kind, and generous behaviors than their peers, a result that is both logically and statistically suspect...Participants consistently overestimated the likelihood that they would act in generous or selfless ways, whereas their predictions of others were considerably more accurate."

Evidence for this effect is everywhere. In a study conducted among faculty members at the University of Nebraska, David Dunning and Justin Kruger found that 68% of professors ranked themselves in the top 25% for teaching ability among their coworkers, and over 90% of them rated themselves as above average.

Speaking of BTAE, I was quite certain of my outstanding abilities when I was 27. I had founded and was running a non-profit that was experiencing noteworthy positive outcomes with gang kids and other struggling children. I felt flattered when asked to speak at a related conference, and it came as no surprise when a few days after the conference, an owner of a large construction company, David Butler, asked if we could meet. He could not have been more affirming of my talk by telling me how "brilliant and insightful" he had found it.

After going on for several minutes about how amazing I was, he asked if he could be totally candid. I had assumed with all the praise he had copiously heaped on me that he was already "being candid." But of course, I was an adult and was interested in his feedback.

Then, with all his broad experience, wealth and influence, he simply said, "Flip, you have to be one of the dumbest people I have ever met when it comes to business." (Just to be clear, I'm not endorsing this as a best practice when giving feedback, but my ego needed that level of candor.)

As my mouth gaped open, he added, "You have a big heart, but you don't have a clue about growing an organization and managing resources." He then added a few more thoughts about how clueless I was, which apparently was going to take some time!

The biggest problem was that he was right. I simply didn't know how bad off I was. I could only see what I could see. Having had success with a lot of struggling kids, I felt like I knew what I was doing.

I had built a Second Story in which I had it all together and didn't need help.

It's easy to understand how thinking you're already above average in everything you do suppresses and prohibits growth. The BTAE can trap you in a cycle of learning the hard way and unnecessarily slow growth.

One of my dearest friends, Dr. Joe Emmert, also has a little bit of BTAE in him. His life mantra should be something like, "If you're going to tell yourself a story, you should at least make it a great one!" My assistant had called him to coordinate a meeting, and since I would be joining the meeting late and she had never met him face-to-face, she asked him how she would be able to recognize him. His response was one he's used hundreds of times. "Well, people say I look a lot like Robert Redford when he was younger. The only difference may be that my build is slightly bigger."

She did her best to keep it together upon meeting my dear, short, somewhat pudgy friend with the most amazing smile and heart. As he says, "If I have to believe something, why not make it something that I like? It works, at least until reality shows up. And besides, being a sex symbol isn't as easy as people think it is!"

WORSE THAN AVERAGE EFFECT

On the other hand, the Worse Than Average Effect (WTAE) can be just as untrue—and damaging. A lot of people dangerously undervalue themselves, often because their First Story filled them with feelings of inadequacy.

All too often, people lie to themselves by confirming the negative information provided by others. Instead of hope, optimism, and determination, we're plagued with feelings of insecurity. In the age of social media, the WTAE has only been fertilized further.

Whether it's photos of exotic vacations, heartfelt declarations of true love, or retouched pictures that remove all blemishes, we feed ourselves a steady diet of other people's highlight reels. The number of likes or number of friends shouldn't be the basis of our value, and yet so many of us struggle with this illusion. We compare our worst to someone else's best and end up feeling even worse (we talk about this further in Story Dragon #2, Chapter 6).

This causes our Second Story to be constructed upon other people's thoughts and opinions about us.

GOING TO HARVARD?

I speak from extensive personal experience on a distorted Second Story. I crafted many of my Second Story lies from a place of fear.

True confession: I was encouraged by a Harvard professor to apply to their Ph.D. program. Guess why I passed on the opportunity:

1. It was too far from home.
2. I couldn't leave my family.
3. I didn't have the proper wardrobe.
4. I could get a doctorate at another university that was just as good as Harvard.

Correct answer? All of the above, *and* none of the above.

I convinced myself those were my reasons while wearing my WTAE glasses, but the real reason I didn't pursue the opportunity was that I was afraid of failing and terrified of being revealed as a fraud for even acting like I could be Ivy League material.

I passed on the opportunity and told myself a story. I'm not alone in that, because we have a story for everything we do. Buy a car, you have a story. Date a person, you tell yourself a story. Leave a relationship, devise a story. Get a job, quit a job, move to that city, etc., there is always a story.

To be clear, I'm not living in the past as I share the Harvard story. We'll cover in the next chapter the importance of focusing on the future. The question shouldn't be, "Wouldn't my life have been better if I had gone to Harvard?" The better question is, "Did I tell myself lies?" Easy answer to that.

You may have noticed how I used my own Second Story as the example for both BTAE and WTAE. Remember that part about how a lot of people struggle with shades of both?

ORGANIZATIONS HAVE SECOND STORIES TOO

I've seen many organizations, whether a school, sports team, family unit, non-profit, or corporation also tell themselves stories, and they can also be BTAE or WTAE versions.

Schools can start to tell themselves that their students just don't get it and don't have the home environments to be able to succeed. Corporations can tell themselves that profits are priority one and then lose sight of a bigger purpose. Families can tell themselves that dysfunctions have run deep for generations and resign themselves to repeating the same patterns.

Organizations write Second Stories and then don't challenge what they've told themselves. Think of all of the businesses that went under because the leaders couldn't change the story they had told themselves, whether it was due to justification or fear of change. Look at current events or challenges in our world today—whatever side you are on or even if you're in the middle, you can see how people tell themselves a story and then look for information to reinforce it.

MAKING EXCUSES

What's interesting is that both BTAE and WTAE strugglers battle making excuses. We make excuses and defend the scripts written to justify where we are and what we do.

- Lost your temper? "They pushed my buttons."
- Failed a math test you didn't study for? "I'm terrible with numbers."
- Got rejected? "I'll never be loved."
- Hurt someone you have power over? "They are too sensitive."
- Received critical feedback from a parent or teacher? "I knew I was bad at..."
- Didn't get enough credit at work? "My supervisor has it in for me."
- In an unhealthy relationship? "It's the best I can do."
- Won't address a conflict in your life? "I'm afraid they'll be upset with me."
- Can't get out of your comfort zone? "That's not natural to me—it wouldn't feel right."

We use our Second Story as a scapegoat to justify our immobility, our arrogance, our crippling anxiety, our conflict avoidance, our fears, our mistakes, our self-critical tendencies, and our jealousy. And if you believe a distortion or lie long enough, it can begin to feel very true.

Some Second Story "Greatest Hits" include:

- Stories that "Keep us from having to change." How many people do you know who have written a victim mindset for themselves? "If only (fill in the blank), then life would have been okay." The list can be endless and the excuses diverse, but the storyline is the same—it's never their fault and they are powerless to do anything about it.
- Stories that "Keep us from failing or taking risks." A high school student shrugs off trying a new sport. One person avoids asking another out on a date. A teacher avoids the

opportunity to be the team leader. The college graduate decides not to book the international flight.

- Stories that "Exaggerate who we are and inflate our abilities." In this version, we scratch and claw for some identity and mask our insecurities by amplifying our competencies. We put on a mask and then deflect any reality-based feedback we receive.

What do all these stories have in common? They're all driven by fear—the fear of vulnerability, failure, exposure, change, and growth. We have stories to justify what we do, and we have stories to justify what we don't do. We have stories that allow us to stay just like we are and feel totally okay doing it.

A young lady once shared that her boyfriend was going to propose to her during the coming weekend. She was excited because he had asked for a specific time to meet. But instead of proposing, he broke up with her. It wasn't at all the story she had told herself.

When she brokenheartedly called a friend to share what had happened, her friend wasn't surprised. "Remember, you said that he would come kicking and screaming to the altar, if he came at all?"

Why tell yourself a story in which you settle for marrying someone who doesn't love you? That young lady could have spent the rest of her life living in an empty marriage.

There's a psychological payoff to our Second Stories: We often do what we do to feel okay with who we are. But there's also a cost: limited growth and never living to your fullest potential.

We all have fears that direct our lives and keep us from changing. Being afraid is perhaps the most common human experience. Think about this: You are born with only two fears— loud noises and falling. All your other fears were learned. Now,

I have a question for you. If the extra fears are learned, can they be unlearned?

Every unchallenged, fear-based script stunts our emotional growth. Each script examined and replaced is a step or a leap toward our best us. You can stay afraid, or you can decide to face your fears, quit telling yourself false stories, and make a change.

CONFIRMATION BIAS

Why can't we see these false stories? For one, we are all prone to confirmation bias, which is our brain's annoying habit of only paying attention to information that confirms our current worldview. Confirmation bias allows us to maintain a faulty perspective even in the midst of evidence to the contrary.

This means we're not as independent as we would like to believe. Biases can shape and cloud our Second Story, which means we have to be vigilant against their effects.

I met recently with my friend, Professor of Cognitive Neuroscience Brian Anderson who said it well: "Your interpretation of what you see is not what is truly there or the totality of what can be seen. You will see what you have trained yourself to see, not with your eyes, but through your interpretation of what you see. That interpretation gives you your perception, and that perception is reshaped by all of the events and inputs and interpretations that have preceded the current input."

When you think about the distortions in your Second Story, here are five questions to reflect on:

1. What story have you told yourself?
2. How do you know that story is true?
3. What other stories/explanations could there be?

4. Do you need to find other people or a different environment to help you see clearly?
5. How would your behavior be different if you let go of any untruths?

THE IMPACT OF ILLUSIONS

In 1983, magician David Copperfield made the 225-ton Statue of Liberty disappear in front of a live audience and on national television. The viewer consensus: "We know the laws of physics say it was impossible, but we saw it with our own eyes!"

Copperfield pulled it off with an illusion which involved raising a curtain to block the audience's view and then rotating the audience seating slowly, all while playing jarring music that masked the vibrations of the shifting seats. When the curtain dropped back down, the audience's line of sight was altered without realizing it.

Close the curtain again, return the seats to the original position, remove the curtain, and Lady Liberty had reappeared.

Copperfield didn't change the New York landscape. He changed the viewpoint.

For our Second Stories, this begs the questions: What distortions appear in the view of your skyline? Has your mental stage been rotated? When will you start challenging the illusions you created or reinforced? It's one thing when we are deceived by a magician, but it's altogether different when we deceive ourselves.

The unfortunate truth is that most of the people you know will live and die within their Second Stories. They either cannot or will not see beyond the illusion they've cobbled together from other people's opinions, expectations, and assessments of their worth. It's heartbreaking when you think about all the things we miss because we tell ourselves stories that aren't true.

There is so much unrealized potential, life, joy, and love buried beneath the rubble of our Second Stories. If we can deconstruct the restrictive lies we tell ourselves about our past and present, we can rework the trajectory of our future.

Are you ready to begin permanently revising and rewriting your Second Story, scene by scene?

It may not always be easy, but the rewards are greater than you ever dreamed because *you* are greater than you ever dreamed.

Recap of Key Points:

- Your Second Story is the one you tell yourself, and it is full of half-truths.
- Your Second Story is often based on learned fears.
- Second Stories can have a Better Than Average Effect (BTAE), a Worse Than Average Effect (WTAE), or a mixture of both.
- We make excuses and tell ourselves lies to make us feel okay.
- You have the power to challenge your Second Story.

Reflection/Discussion Questions:

- Which item in the "Recap of Key Points" jumps out at you the most?
- Is your Second Story the more inflated (BTAE) or suppressed (WTAE) version—or some of both?
- What's a specific excuse or justification you've made in the past? Why do you think you made the excuse?
- What is a lie you told yourself based on your First or Second Story? (e.g., about your abilities, your potential, or decisions you've made)
- How would your behavior be different if you removed some of your Second Story distortions?
- Who would be an honest sounding board to discuss your Second Story with?

CHAPTER 4

YOUR THIRD STORY: THE ONE YOU WRITE

"When writing the story of your life, don't let anyone else hold the pen."

- Unknown

YOU CAN PICK YOUR FRAME

My grandmother was a talented artist. She loved art.

When I was a young boy, a woman brought over a painting for my grandmother to look at. I walked into the living room and saw the painting leaning against the wall. My grandmother sat across the room, staring intensely at this abstract painting that made no sense to me at all.

"Sonny," my grandmother asked, "What do you think about this piece of art?"

"That's got to be the ugliest thing I've ever seen," I replied.

My grandmother slowly walked up to it, picked it up, and turned it over on its side. I still couldn't even tell which way was up! After pondering the piece, she said, "Well, it just needs a new frame."

Then you'll just have an ugly picture in a nice frame, I thought.

When I visited her a few weeks later, the painting had a new frame and my grandmother asked, "Doesn't it look better?"

"Oh wow, it really does," I said. And it was true. With a new frame, the painting was much more captivating to look at.

That memory stuck with me. The painting didn't change, but different lighting, fresh surroundings, and even the varying moods of viewers drastically affected its appearance.

So much of our life is that way, too. Events in our lives may initially appear a certain way to us, but we still have the power to reframe them. And remember, we didn't paint many of the originals.

A LIFE WITHOUT NEED TO REFRAME?

You wouldn't think Scotty Smiley would need to reframe anything:

- In high school he wanted to make the honor roll. Done.
- He wanted to be captain of his high school football team and take them to the state championship. He did.
- He wanted to go to West Point. Ditto.

- He wanted to marry his high school sweetheart. She said, "Yes."
- He wanted to be a combat-diver qualified infantryman and get accepted to Ranger School. Check.

We had met briefly before, but when a stay-off-the-roads blizzard shut down Pasco, Washington and gave him unexpected downtime, we got together to talk in more detail. "Flip, ask whatever you want," he started, "I'm fine talking about it with you."

"It" was an April 2005 morning in Mosul, Iraq when his life trajectory was blown apart. He found himself staring down a potential car bomber with no idea that would be the last thing he ever saw.

He had flagged down an old Opel car and ordered the driver to exit with arms over his head because the rear of the car was sagging, a sign of heavy explosives. When the driver shook his head "no" and took his foot off the brake, Scotty fired three warning shots in front of the vehicle.

"That's when he detonated the car," Scotty said.

One piece of shrapnel cut his left eye in two and lodged into his frontal lobe, while other pieces destroyed his right eye and peppered his face. When he regained consciousness a week later, he was 6,000 miles away in the Walter Reed Army Medical Center with his wife, Tiffany, at his bedside.

Everything he knew and believed—his entire Second Story— was as shattered as that Opel. If you work hard, live right, date the right person, make the right decisions and get the right level of education, you would be successful and happy.

Now Scotty couldn't do anything on his own—couldn't find clothes and had no idea what he looked like in them even if he could, couldn't shave, couldn't brush his teeth and couldn't turn on music.

His Second Story was amazing, until it wasn't. It obviously wasn't going as planned—most stories seldom do.

"I was so angry I even denied God," Scotty explained. "I thought I had earned the right to a good life. Now I would never see my wife's face again, half of my body was temporarily paralyzed, and I felt like I would never live any of my dreams. I was in a dark place, developed PTSD, jumped at loud noises and had horrific nightmares for a year and a half."

"Going through the process of writing my Third Story brought up a lot of things I had never considered," he remembered. "I realized that first I needed to forgive myself because I made a lot of decisions that led to that hospital bed. I chose to go to West Point, chose to go into the infantry, and chose to use my rifle instead of kneeling down behind the 50mm machine gun mounted on my Stryker vehicle. But I couldn't move on to happiness and have a purposeful life if I hung on to regret and resentment."

"It was not one big moment or epiphany where God brought me back, it was actually a million tiny ones—the first time I was able to get dressed on my own, when I got the first whiff of Tiffany's perfume again, or the day I learned I would be able to return to active duty," he recalled with a smile. "I learned that no one does it on their own. True success happens when you learn to rely on others."

SMALL STEPS ADD UP

One step at a time, he emphasized with me. Turns out those small steps covered a lot of distance.

Scotty became the first blind, active duty officer in U.S.

Army history. He earned his MBA from Duke University, taught at West Point and was selected the *Army Times* 2007 U.S. Army Soldier of the Year.

He skydived, skied down Colorado mountains, surfed in Hawaii, climbed Mount Rainer, and completed the Coeur d'Alene Ironman triathlon. His buddies, officers Jeff and Luke Van Antwerp and their dad Lieutenant General "Van" Van Antwerp and many other amazing people encouraged and challenged him every day. But the truth is, he challenged them as well. Who wants to ski with a blind guy chasing you down a mountain and trying to beat you? All of this explains why he won a 2008 ESPY award as the Best Outdoor Athlete!

Since Army retirement in 2015 and against long odds, he has had a rich and rewarding life. He travels cross-country to New York City in his job as an investment banker for organizations around the world. More importantly, there is Tiffany and their three sons—Grady Douglas, Graham Elliott, and Baylor Scott. "I've never seen the boys' faces and I never will see my beautiful wife Tiffany's face again," he said matter-of-factly.

Then I got personal: "How does Tiffany's face feel?"

Scotty sat quietly. I could almost see inside his mind as he painted a picture from memory. "Tiffany's face is gorgeous. It's soft. She has high cheek bones with a dimple on one cheek, a little nose and small ears. Her lips are full, and her teeth are amazing when she smiles. Almond shaped, bright blue eyes and across her nose little freckles that I always loved—and still love. They darken in the summer. It's a beautiful, beautiful face."

"How do the faces of your sons feel?" I asked.

"Each boy is different. It's fun to feel the changes as they go through stages of growth, chubby at first then they thin out. Grady is thinner with a chiseled face, little chin and ears. He has high cheekbones, a smaller nose and lots of hair. Graham has a rounder face, bigger ears, bigger nose. He smiles all the time and has joyful, happy eyebrows. Baylor has a chubbier face because he's only six. He has beautiful middle-sized ears, nose, and mouth. His eyes sparkle and when he smiles, he doesn't show much teeth—just grins ear-to-ear. I've become a touchy, feeling guy. It's how I express and experience love."

What a special blessing he has found in blindness. In that moment I was glad Scotty couldn't see me sitting quietly as tears ran down my face. I wondered how well I could answer my own question. What does Susan's face feel like? What do my sons' faces feel like? What do my grandchildren's faces feel like? What do they smell like and what do their faces do when they smile?

He and Tiffany go all over the country sharing their story—their Third Story. The one they chose to write and reframe so beautifully.

When asked if he could get a "do over" of that fateful day in Mosul, he answered, "I wouldn't change a thing, not even being blinded. Obviously, there are significant good things I miss out on. But I refuse to focus on what I don't have. I have an amazing wife, children I treasure, a wonderful home, and a great career. I focus on the goodness of life, and I get to use my gifts to benefit my family and others. I wouldn't give that up just to get my vision back."

Looking beyond his blindness has let him see lots of things most of us don't.

CAN YOU CONTROL YOUR PAST?

Did you know that your memories aren't really your memories? Many of them are just complex reflections of the people who wrote on you.

But they aren't fixed or static. They're malleable. Memories are also not as accurate as we like to think. That is why eyewitness testimonies aren't always reliable evidence in a court of law. When we tell a story or remember an important moment from our lives, our brains don't recall everything exactly as it happened. Instead, we remember certain parts that stand out. If we've told the story before, we amp up some elements based on our current feelings and any reactions we've received from others.

The way we choose to imprint memories and retell them reshapes the stories themselves by modifying the strength and interconnectedness of neural pathways in our brain. Scotty Smiley is a prime example of how we have a remarkable ability to shape our perception of the past by how we think and talk about it.

Sometimes, it can be incredibly difficult to find the good. What if you experienced something hurtful? What if you were rejected by someone you loved? What if your parents are divorced? What if you lost your job? How could anything constructive come out of our pain and fears?

The event itself may have been a hard experience, but you can choose to find something positive.

Perhaps the pain you experienced created internal strength and character development that have become valuable parts of who you are. Or the hardship gave you a heightened sensitivity to others' experiences. Maybe it got you out of a complacent status quo, or maybe it made you appreciate some things you took for granted.

My wife Susan and I have both had painful things happen in our lives. I could easily choose to be bitter or think that life isn't fair and resent some of my difficult experiences. Or I can be thankful for how those experiences have been a catalyst for good and how they allowed me to feel what so many others feel on a much deeper level. Reframing the bad in your life and finding the good is a powerful way to build resilience and think beyond your present circumstances. This process can't erase the real-world events of the past, but it does allow us to construct a new frame around how we view those events.

Which brings us to another friend, Colt McCoy. A lot of incredible people wrote on young Colt, giving him solid values and a great childhood. As a high school quarterback, he ran up a 34-2 record (and rumor has it his teachers said he never made below 95 on a test). Life was good.

He went on to college and was a four-year starter at the University of Texas, walking off the field with 45 wins, which at the time was the most career wins ever for a college quarterback. In the process, he set and still holds the career completion percentage record (76.7%). As a college senior, Colt won 13 of the top 15 major player awards, including quarterback of the year, offensive player of the year, and outstanding football player of the year. Twice he was a finalist for the Heisman Trophy.

When I said I bet most people looked at him and saw a young man with few regrets or concerns or worries, he agreed. "I think you're right," he continued, "but they don't see the reality that I still have internal struggles to overcome. Just like everyone else."

A CHAMPIONSHIP MOMENT

One of those inner struggles assaulted him as he stood in the brightest spotlight of his life, the 2009 NCAA championship game against Alabama. That January night in the Rose Bowl, on Texas' first possession, he was impressively driving the Longhorns toward the goal line when he got hit. Hard.

The hit spiked a nerve in his shoulder, numbing his right arm all the way to his hand. When he tried to throw, he couldn't grip the ball. He could still throw with velocity using his arm strength—he just had no control over where it would go. His team would not get that national championship.

Most people could identify with the pain of losing a dream. But who would have guessed that underneath that injury was an inner voice in Colt insisting, "You should be ashamed. Look at all the people you let down."

His own frustration and pain were multiplied because, "I hurt for everyone knowing what we could have accomplished." His Second Story was telling him that real champions never let people down as he walked gingerly out of the Rose Bowl "knowing" he was a loser.

"Even though I didn't recognize it fully," Colt continued, "my Second Story was saying that if you don't win the national championship, no one will ever appreciate you like they would have if you were a winner."

Fortunately, he eventually realized what everyone else knew. "I didn't win that game, but that doesn't define me. I can still carry my head high. I can't control everything and tell the stars how to align." Or tell an Alabama linebacker not to unload on you full force.

His Third Story rewrite served him well in coming to terms with that loss, and it has proven invaluable on a decade-long NFL journey. Over the next nine years, Colt lined up under center in Cleveland, in San Francisco, and in Washington. But he wasn't winning championships or even starting—and not many people felt he could. In 2018, he had another chance and was making the most of it. A huge story in the *Washington Post* chronicled "Colt McCoy's path from Browns castoff to scout team legend to the most important player on the Redskins."

Given the unexpected chance to play when the starting quarterback went down, he seized it and played really well. But in the second quarter against the Philadelphia Eagles, he got hit. Hard. (Sound familiar?) Though the fibula in his right leg was fractured, he stayed in the game for the last two plays of the series—and completed both passes.

The details were different, but he said it felt a lot like his last college game. Except for one major thing. Frustration? Yes. Disappointment? Yes. Shame? Not this time. The hurt was deep and wide. He still wanted to meet others' expectations if he could. But he wasn't ashamed.

"It was my fifth year in the Washington system. I felt comfortable with our offense. I worked really hard behind the scenes to have the opportunity to play again. The team and coaches believed in me because they had seen me working every day. I stepped in and played well. Then, just like that, it's over."

"My Third Story is not even close to written," he told me, "but this part will help me deal with other challenges—like when someone tells me I'm not good enough to play at this level anymore. That won't be the end of a productive life. I've got other talents and other interests."

Not that he plans on reaching that point anytime soon. "I really like the country song 'Five More Minutes.' After losing his last high school football game, the quarterback wants to deny reality, pleading with his coach that the 'next time to get in here I'll have to buy a ticket. Can't you give me five more minutes?'"

"That pretty much tells the tale for professional athletes when they retire," Colt added. "They can't figure out how to get that feeling from anything else. Where are they going to find meaning for the next 50 years of their lives? They won't find out unless they learn how to write their Third Story." The good news is that they are competitors and have the ability, if they translate it from their athletic drive, to write a great Third Story. Just like Colt.

And like Colt, you can't write the beginning to your life or even some parts in the middle, but you can sure write the ending. You just have to learn how.

FOUR STORY-WRITING TRUTHS

There are some things I have learned about writing our stories, both as a psychotherapist from talking with thousands of patients and from later consulting work. Before you write your Third Story, you need to embrace the four story-writing truths:

1. You are not who you could be (yet!).
2. Your self-talk needs some rewiring.
3. You need an emotionally compelling reason to change.
4. You can't help yourself by yourself.

YOU ARE NOT WHO YOU COULD BE (YET!)

This is an absolute truth you must embrace. You are more than you could ever imagine. There is more depth, more ability, more talent, more love, more goodness, more opportunity, and more of everything than you could ever dream possible.

Who you are now is not the total picture of who you can become. If you can't accept this, then we have a problem. Actually, you have a problem. But the problem is fixable! I have never met anyone who is fully who they are capable of being. That's great news. It means there is more, no matter how satisfied you are. There is more because you are more.

YOUR SELF-TALK NEEDS SOME REWIRING

Yes, you talk to yourself. And you listen to what you say. Maybe not out loud, but self-talk is the running commentary in your head. When self-talk is negative, you hear things like:

- I can't...
- There I go again...
- That was all my fault...
- Others are better than I am...
- I messed that up again...
- I can't believe I did...
- I don't deserve...
- I knew I shouldn't have tried to...
- I'll never...

My co-author Chris teaches self-talk skills while coaching his kids' athletic teams. Every year, he asks the same question at the first practice: "Who is the toughest opponent we are going to face this year?"

Without hesitation, they usually growl the name of a rival team and Chris quickly retorts, "Nope." Or his players name a dominant player from the previous year. "No, that player won't be our toughest opponent."

Is our toughest opponent our coaches? "Very funny!" Chris says, "but wrong!" After several incorrect answers a player will eventually guess, "Ourselves?"

Chris will smile and reply, "Yes, that's it! The toughest opponent we'll face looks right back at us in the mirror!"

If we can get the person in the mirror to be on our side, we are a long way down the path to our Third Story.

YOU NEED AN EMOTIONALLY COMPELLING REASON TO CHANGE

If you want to rewrite intentionally, you need an emotionally compelling reason to drive that change. Even a large dose of facts, philosophy, or logic won't "git 'er done" as a solo change agent. Logic stacks the wood, but emotion lights the fire. For both me and my friend Pat Wadors, one of the most emotional torches was having kids.

The day I took my firstborn son, Matthew, home from the hospital, I sat on the backyard grass and held him in my lap. With my hand on his tiny chest I vowed, "Matthew, I will change everything in my life that needs to change so that you can become the man you are intended to become."

I had an emotionally compelling reason to change my default parenting style—my son deserved it. That was my commitment then, and I have repeated that birthday commitment every year since. Today all of my sons are grown with their own families, but my children know my commitment to them is constant.

Pat's spark came from commitment to her son too. Taking time off from work to see your son's first Little League baseball game or nurse him when he's sick is not often seen as a way to advance your business career.

This is especially true when you are a senior executive in a fast-growing company. Pat, current Chief Talent Officer at Service Now and former Senior Vice President at LinkedIn, doesn't have time to waste, but she carved just enough out of her schedule explain how the clash between the demands of her budding career and mom duty launched her Third Story.

"My emotionally compelling reason came in early motherhood when I became the sole breadwinner," she explained. After her husband quit his job to stay home so she could pursue her dream,

"I felt my shoulders get broader; I felt my body shift because I was taking more risks and feeling more fear."

Her Second Story argued against taking chances. "My past was rough. I had a learning disability and my parents thought I was just lazy. I excelled at sports and art, though," before adding humorously, "because you don't have to spell or do math to do those well!"

Women in the workplace don't let mommy duty invade the office. But Pat did take that chance—and got noticed. The more she did, the more other women would ask, "How do you do that?" And the more they asked, the more fear she felt.

When she sought counsel on this, a mentor asked a very focused question: "Who and where do you want to be years from now?" That was easy. "I want to run a human resources division. I'm here to serve others."

"When will you know you have made it?" the mentor inquired.

"When I'm a 70-year-old woman with colorful hair and funky clothes who champions the talent around me while being fun to hang out with," she replied.

Then she couldn't help but ask herself, "Why wait? I can be that person right now."

It worked. As her career bloomed, "people trusted me more because they could sense that I was real."

Years later, Pat still preaches what she practices, encouraging corporate executives to spend time with their families and be true to who they really are, because "there is measurable correlation between a person being real and their being more productive and staying with the company longer."

But wait, there's more.

"When you manage with this emphasis, that's real success.

You not only touch the employee's life but also their family's," she insisted. "Multiply the number of people in front of you by five."

That's some real math. The kind that really counts in writing our Third Stories.

YOU CAN'T HELP YOURSELF BY YOURSELF

I'll talk in more detail about this in Step 3 of the next chapter, but this truth is worth repeating: You can't do this alone. You need other people.

I've had a lot of life challenges I fought with for years—many of which were inside my head. And the challenges and stresses didn't get much better or clearer there. I already knew my perspective, so I just further reinforced any distortions. Let me expound on this a little more. At times you may think you "changed your mind," but in reality all you likely did was rearrange what was already there. When there is a real change, there is almost always some outside help. You have to include other people in your Third Story journey. The trick is finding the right ones.

So, if you said "amen" to those four story-writing truths, you're on your way to authoring a successful Third Story.

FRAMES COME IN SIZE SMALL TOO

As I write this, I'm returning from an Alaskan fishing trip with two of my grandsons. Every night during our adventure, I would ask them, "What good things happened to you today? What are you thankful for tonight?"

You would think it would be easy to come up with several good things you're thankful for when you're fishing the Alaskan countryside on Granddad's dime. But reframing and thankfulness are learned behaviors.

Sometimes it was like pulling teeth. By the third night, it started getting a little easier. Let me share with you how Dylan responded to every negative I could throw at him.

"It rained all day today." "Yes, but we were fishing in Alaska!"

"We didn't catch any big ones." "Nope, but we caught a lot of other sizes!"

"A bear came out behind you." (really happened) "I got to see a live bear!"

"The room we were in was really cold." "Yeah, but we didn't have to sleep outside!"

Nothing is too small to reframe. How do you reframe making the "B" team instead of the "A" team while not losing your competitiveness? You focus on the fact that you'll get more playing time and that this will push you harder.

A friend of mine, Audra Walsh, posted on social media that she got a flat tire and was stranded with her two young kids. She had no choice but to pull over next to a Burger King. Not long after, the kids started complaining about being hungry, so she relented and went inside to eat. After devouring a burger and fries, son Eli said, "Mom, we are having a very lucky day!" When they finally got home, daughter Adalee excitedly told her dad, Kyle, "Dad, we got to eat at Burger King today and it's my favorite restaurant now!" Audra's kids made her laugh, and they taught her some valuable reframing lessons.

There's more to their story, too. Kyle excelled in sports until he was paralyzed in an auto accident on his way back to practice on the University of Texas football team. He has been in a wheelchair his entire adult life. But today he coaches football, and his team at College Station High School just won the Texas state championship. His attitude is amazing and infectious. One day during practice, he was on the field in his chair when the team ran a sweep around his side. As they plowed over him, he was completely thrown from his wheelchair. When the boys bent over to see how he was, he joked, "Hey, just because I can't feel that doesn't mean that didn't hurt!"

So many people think they have problems until they realize they really don't. As the philosopher Seneca said, "A good person dyes events with his own color…and turns whatever happens to his own benefit."

What if you get poor service at a restaurant? Maybe the chef or attendants are having a hard time in their personal lives, and because you show patience, it spares them additional stress.

What if someone in your family says something hurtful to you? By not firing back, you strengthen your let-it-roll-off muscles and also learn a great example of what not to say to others.

Chris and I attended a funeral recently; our friend's son died tragically. There is nothing that will take away that pain or bring him back. I visited with James and sat quietly as he cried over his son's death. Then he said the most beautiful things. "We only had him for 19 years. I wouldn't trade any of that time, even knowing that I would lose him. I wish I had 19 more, but I'm really going to celebrate the fact that I had him for 19. He was a gift from God, and I will hold onto that gift forever."

All of us, at some time in our lives, will have to learn how to reframe parts of our stories. If you don't, it will not be your best story. It's not easy, but it can be learned and practiced. You can almost always find something to be thankful for, and if you can't at first, learn to look more deeply. There is likely something you missed.

PROBE DAY IS A GREAT DAY

My friend, Eric Lokey, has had some bumps in his journey. A regular occurrence for him is "probe day"—the day they stick needles and tubes in him to determine if his cancer has returned. His wife, Debi, wrote me after one of the probe days. "This is a great day. We didn't think he would even be here five years after the diagnosis. Every day is so special."

Eric and Debi's Third Stories have become semi-automatic— less focus on needles and tubes, and more focus on finding the good. They are an amazing couple and have been sweethearts since they were kids, but they have found more. Every day is precious and to watch them, you would think it was the best day ever. You can do that too, if you choose to. Take hold of your fears, worries, failures, pains, and future. Learn to control them so they don't control you.

Ask yourself: Could I be more? Do I want to be more?

Who you are currently is not who you could become. Be the writer of your own story and not just the reader. The next chapter will help you do just that.

Recap of Key Points:

- You can reframe and find the good.
- You are not who you could be (yet!).
- Your self-talk needs some rewiring.
- We are often our toughest opponent.
- You need an emotionally compelling reason to change.
- You can't help yourself by yourself.
- You are more.

Reflection/Discussion Questions:

- Which item in the "Recap of Key Points" jumps out at you the most?
- What's an event in your life that would benefit from a different frame?
- On a 1 to 10 scale, how constructive is your self-talk?
- What's an emotionally compelling reason that could spur you to change?
- Who is someone who could help you navigate your Third Story?
- What's the cost of not rewriting your story?

CHAPTER 5

WRITE YOUR THIRD STORY: BUILD A STORY PLAN

"Nobody can go back and start a new beginning,
but anyone can start today and make a new ending."
- Maria Robinson

In the last chapter, we presented and defined what a Third Story is. Now we'll get started writing your Third Story in five basic steps. You can capture your answers to each step on the Story Plan at the end of this chapter.

STEP 1: WHAT'S YOUR WHAT?

To answer this question, don't just think about who others want you to be, what you think would make everyone else happy, or even what you have always done. Start by thinking about these questions:

- What type of key relationships do you want?
- What's a goal you want to achieve?
- What family dynamic do you want?
- What career do you want?
- How healthy do you want to be?

One coworker told me, "I want to like how I look and be as healthy as I can be."

Another friend wrote, "I want to live out my mission with a great team, doing great things in our arena while building a great company in the process."

And a teacher said, "I want to change future generations by impacting the young people of this generation."

To clarify, I'm not talking about something you might "like" to have or be or do. It's not about "shoulds" or "coulds" or "maybes."

WHAT do you really want?

What do YOU really want?

What do you REALLY want?

It's good to stop and think about the different roles you play. In one important role of mine, I want to be a great husband. I want Susan to be happy and to experience the joy and fulfillment that comes with being adored. I want her to have what she did not have as a child: unconditional, unfettered, reckless, crazy love.

One of my favorite memories is when Susan and I were standing on a sidewalk in New York City, soaked by the driving rain and the splashes of water thrown by cars. Unexpectedly and a bit uncharacteristically, I asked, "May I have this dance?" Then

I took her hand, walked her into the intersection on Wall Street and waltzed in the rain. A few drivers honked and some sidewalk passersby clapped. Think about it—how many guys get to dance with their girl on Wall Street? Sopping wet, we had a blast.

In addition, I want to be a great dad, friend, employer, and colleague. I want to have a company filled with great friends who have a *great* impact. I want to live a life filled with grace and truth and kindness and service. My list is not about boats or trains or planes. It's not about *having* more; it's about *being* more.

I hope you are getting the message here. You have to know what *you* want.

My colleague Chad has a specific "What"—to climb all the "14ers" in Colorado. A 14er is a mountain taller than 14,000 feet, and there are 53 of them in Colorado. He is well on his way, and his 12- and 10-year-old sons have joined him. I suspect those boys will become men on those mountains.

The "What" works in schools, too.

Arrow's Liberation Academy is located outside of Houston, Texas, and is led by Drs. Audrey Sanders and Jim Christensen. They decided their "What" would be, "No child should be trapped by the zip code their family lives in—we will create a school in which every child receives a quality education, is loved, and becomes successful."

That's a "What" that can change lives. And they didn't just want it, they *really* wanted it.

After much diligence and hard work, their school was honored as a *Capturing Kids' Hearts National Showcase School* and a National Blue Ribbon School, being ranked #13 out of over 9,000 Texas schools in closing the achievement gap over a five-year period. In fact, they wanted their "What" so badly, they just visited the White House for a celebration of these accomplishments.

Their "What" is changing lives, indeed!

STEP 2: WHAT'S YOUR WHY?

Next, you need to ask yourself why you want the things on your "What" list. Most successful individuals can answer the "Why" question quickly; they usually have a deep sense of why they do what they do.

Since everyone's "Why" is not created equal, be sure to look for emotionally compelling reasons for aspiring for things you want. When I asked an audience of college students in London why they were enrolled in one of the top universities in the world, one student sitting in the front answered, "I really want a good job."

"Why do you want a good job?" I asked.

"I want to be able to buy a car and other things," he answered.

"So, let me get this straight," I said. "You invested four years of your life and a small fortune in your education, all so you can buy a car. Is that what you just told me?" I smiled and added, "Wouldn't there have been an easier way to get a car?" Of course, everyone laughed. We had a fun time together, but the truth is that he didn't have a very good "Why."

At the other end of the "Why" spectrum is Alex Navab. In 1979, a three-hour flight from Iran to Greece transformed 14-year-old Alex from a comfortable life of "have" to an uprooted "have not."

With the Iranian revolution well under way, his father decided for the sake of his family to abandon a comfortable and prestigious life as dean of the Isfahan University of Medical Sciences. That meant also abandoning everything else that wouldn't cram into a few suitcases.

When they arrived at the airport, Alex's dad was being questioned before boarding the plane. As officials separated his dad from the family, their greatest fears were realized. His family could leave, but he had to remain.

Can you imagine the emotions as their family was ripped apart? Through the daze, Alex heard his father's parting words: "Alex you are the oldest. Take care of everyone until I can be with you." As the guards led his father away, the teenager staggered under the thought that he might never see his father again.

From that moment on, Alex had a compelling "What" and "Why." What did he want? He wanted to take care of his family and keep them safe. Why? Because his father asked him to and there was no other alternative if they were to make it. Two years later, his father was allowed out of the country and reunited with the family in Greece. Not long after that, they emigrated to the United States.

I wish you could have been with me to hear his detailed story as his wife, Mary Kathryn, and their children affectionately sat close to him on the couch in their living room. His emotionally compelling "Why"—caring for others—has continued in his position as one of the top investment managers in the world.

Despite being a partner at one of the top private equity firms in the world, he knew there was more he wanted to do, he just wasn't sure what that was. After considerable discussion and reflection, he told me, "I know where my next story lies. I'm starting my own firm: Navab Capital Partners." With his unprecedented focus on corporate philanthropy, we were both excited about the possibilities ahead.

Alex's amazing Third Story is only getting better. He is now poised to launch the largest first fund in private equity history as he conscientiously stewards his clients' money, pensions, futures, and dreams. And in the process, he cares for his family, as well.

(NOTE: The week this book was going to print, my dear friend Alex Navab passed away at the age of 53. He was writing his life's Third Story and could not have been more excited about all he was working on. I was honored to know him and love him. He leaves a great story and a powerful legacy with his family—one filled with joy, a passion for life, and a deep love for each of them. Remember that life is short; let's all dream bigger and know that when it ends, we have lived large. Like Alex.)

STEP 3: WHO'S YOUR WHO?

You'll remember from the last chapter that you can't help yourself by yourself. You need other people at your side and on your side.

A famed bit of folk wisdom advises that the first thing to do when you find yourself in a hole is to stop digging. That's a good point, but hardly a complete action plan. Even if you stop digging, you are still in the pits. So as soon as you quit digging—and before that, if possible—start yelling, "Somebody get me out of here!" Then be open to listening and learning.

We all need mentors and other helpers to see our way out of the pit. But there are some dangers to avoid as you identify "Who" will mentor you:

- Don't expect a single mentor to advise across all areas of your life.
- Don't expect mentors to track you down or follow up.
- Don't think mentoring you is the only appointment on their calendars.
- Don't seek a mentor to simply validate your existing opinions.

What if you don't have a clear "Who" candidate? Just look around and ask yourself a few questions. Who is living a life worth living? Who is someone that makes solid decisions? Who are some people who seem to really care?

Watch how they deal with mistakes…and success. How do they treat other people? How do they treat you? Do they help you sort through ideas without killing your creativity? Can they pull the "weeds" in your life without pulling up the "flowers" too? Do they believe you have something to contribute and abilities worth sharing? Do you feel inspired and hope-filled when with them?

Fortunately, as a skilled hole digger, I learned the need for help early on and unashamedly pursued amazing mentors like Bob Wood and federal Judge Woodrow Seals. These men had a profound impact in my life and came into my life because I asked them to help me get better. I owe much of my professional career to these advisors.

I mentioned David Butler in Chapter 3 and how he challenged me on a lack of business knowledge. He went on to mentor me for years as a trusted friend and advisor. Every Wednesday, he asked me to solve difficult business problems before patiently walking me through solutions. David said he wanted to invest in me because his days were numbered.

One Wednesday he called and said he couldn't meet. "Flip, you are good," he said. "You are going to be okay. You've gotten pretty smart now!" He passed away that Saturday night, leaving behind a family that loved him and others, like me, with a deep imprint on our lives.

Many of my other mentors are much younger than me, as wisdom doesn't come with a time stamp. Pride is the only thing that would keep you from learning from a younger person. And since wisdom is also not gender specific, several of my truth tellers and mentors are women.

WHAT DO YOU DO WITH BAD "WHOS"?

If you have a substandard "Who" in your life, be careful labeling them as all bad. Even the people in my life who hurt me had some positive traits that were easy to overlook. Maybe a parent overuses a strength of attention to detail by nitpicking you, but there's still some good in their attention to detail.

If you've been hurt by someone, you may need to limit your exposure to them. Like my friend who refuses to watch the evening news—at some point, she decided the added negativity was too much to handle and is being more selective with what she lets into her mind. Sometimes you can't change the channel on people in your life, so if you can't set time boundaries with them, at least turn down the volume. Don't let their issues become your issues. And as with anyone who pushes your buttons, hunt for the hidden lesson. What could this person be teaching you? Is there a button they are exposing that others could find in the future? How can you get stronger in the meantime?

Who is your "Who?" Or at least who could be your "Who?" Identify one or two people to share some of your Third Story insights and put their names on your Story Plan. Find a healthy group or community you can plug into, otherwise several years from now you'll still be looking up from the same hole.

STEP 4: WHAT'S YOUR HOW?

1. Believe you can be different.
2. Write a story line.
3. Do some reflecting.
4. Forgive.
5. Reframe your pain.

BELIEVE YOU CAN BE DIFFERENT

This may seem unnecessary, but it's a crucial first part of Step 4. Do you really believe you can redeem and rewrite parts of your story? If so, proceed! If not, look a little harder. Maybe you have some Second Story lies still lurking around. (I told you they were slippery!)

WRITE A STORY LINE

Think for a minute about a Story Line—a statement that encapsulates who you are or who you want to be. It could be something you are learning, a belief you are reinforcing, a lie you are going to stop telling yourself, or something you are unlearning. It could stem from a specific event or be centered around a belief you held or need to hold tighter. It could be an inspiring mantra you want to further internalize. It could be about your future or about a fear you are releasing.

Here are some Story Lines that might have your name on them:

- "I will reframe failure as an amazing chance to learn."
- "I will quit living in fear of making a mistake."
- "I will be the author of my story."
- "I will not be dependent on having a boyfriend/girlfriend."
- "I will stop depending on approval from others."
- "Because I wasn't encouraged, I will be a key encourager for others."
- "I will create a home life where kids feel loved."
- "I will let the right people get closer to me."
- "I will stop making self-limiting statements."
- "I will be more intentional to write good things on others."
- "I will ask more people to challenge the story I've told myself—and then I will listen."
- "I will find more people who can write on me and help me believe in myself."

Once you have it, write your Story Line on your Story Plan at the end of this chapter.

DO SOME REFLECTING

Stopping to smell the roses does more than take you to a happy place. It also gives you the opportunity to spot a few thorns you might have overlooked, whether your reflection is mental, verbal, or written. We live in an age of busyness and packed schedules, so it's important to set aside moments to pause and examine your story.

The night after a friend cared enough to speak the truth about my fear of attending Harvard, I listed in my journal the lies I told myself, one by one. Next, I looked for other areas in my life where similar untruths held me down. Finally, I wrote, in big letters: "I am going to do my best to *never* let my fears dictate my decisions."

I try to pause and write down insights about myself several times a year. I ponder the decisions I made (good or bad), the things I said or didn't say to myself, the people I helped or ignored, and I boil the thoughts down to written form. It's often easier to spot our lies when they're written down. When I was going through a rough patch in my twenties, I remember writing down how I felt about myself. The words were dark: insufficient, failure, not smart enough, unlovable. On the next page, I focused on writing the truth: work in progress, learning, worthy of love, capable.

One reason writing is helpful is that it makes you reflect. It's much less about the journaling and more about the pausing. Also, there is good reflection and not-so-good reflection. Good reflection looks forward, not just backward. Good reflection sees the lessons in the mistakes. Not-so-good reflection lives in the land of forever-lost opportunities. Have you ever wondered how much regret weighs? It would be better to put the weight aside and walk on.

Here are a few other "DON'Ts" when reflecting:

- DON'T get caught up in blaming yourself or others (avoid the victim mindset).
- DON'T dwell (reflecting shouldn't be all-consuming and indefinite).
- DON'T ignore corrections or suggestions others have shared (we need outside input).

Also, don't get hamstrung by the term "journal." My colleague, Joy, likes to journal but sometimes gets intimidated by the "ghosts of English teachers past." She has to give herself permission to just write. She told me, "I'm the only grader of my journal, so I get a grade of 100 on every entry!" Whether it's unclear thoughts, misspellings, or tangents, that's okay, she just knows it's helpful to write.

Another colleague of mine, Karen, sends herself texts as a form of writing/journaling. Another friend uses a notes app. Whatever works for you, do it!

Some examples of topics to write/journal about:

- What's a fear you have? Did fear of failure keep you from attempting something or stepping into the spotlight?
- Have there been times you lied to yourself? We correct children for lying, but don't always apply the same standards to ourselves.
- What are your core beliefs? What deeper beliefs do you have about yourself?
- What do you value? What is important to you, and why?

FORGIVE

Think for a second—who is usually the hardest person to forgive?

For a lot of people, the answer is ourselves. A key step in your Third Story is to go ahead and make the often-overdue decision to forgive yourself.

Why is this so hard? First, because we think we don't deserve it. Repeat after me, "I am human." Humans make mistakes—no exceptions. Since we're all imperfect, we all need forgiveness.

Second, it's hard because we think forgiving means we have to have total peace about something. You might still have some lingering pain or consequences from a past mistake, but forgiving yourself is about finding a way to look forward. Focus on what you can control. You can't change the past, but you can stop looking back at it, and you can choose to forgive yourself.

Of course we have to forgive others, too (more on this in Story Dragon #5 in the next chapter). Forgiveness doesn't mean spending more time with the person who hurt you or losing all boundaries. It's more about letting go mentally so that it doesn't consume you. Holding tightly onto unforgiveness usually just hurts the person gripping it.

REFRAME YOUR PAIN

In a keynote once, my co-author Chris asked the audience to think about some of the demoralizing dips in their life—a mistake made, conflict experienced, a continually unmet expectation, or a strained relationship.

"Now," Chris said, "While thinking about specific dips in your life, I want you to call out the raw emotions that come to mind. What words does that event evoke?"

After a few moments of silence, someone chimed in, "Pain."

Another said, "Guilt."

Another, "Loneliness."

Another, "What if?"

Another, "Regret."

The common underlying theme was clear. But then someone added, "Opportunity." Someone else said, "Growth." A person who had shared a more negative word earlier said, "Stronger," and another, "Thankful."

The good news is that we get to decide which words describe our dips. Clearly, some dips are harder than others, so you may have to look more diligently for the good.

The only way to reclaim is to reframe. When one of my best friends was dying, his wife, Nancy, sent me a plea to come and be with them. But my schedule was packed, so I planned to come visit the next weekend. He died before Friday came.

Nancy wanted me present when he died; I asked her for forgiveness, and through tears she forgave me. I vowed never to delay support I was able to give to people who needed me. And in a way I never expected, that resolve was tested. Nancy eventually remarried another close friend of mine. Ten years later, he was tragically killed in a car crash. I was there for Nancy then. And she didn't have to ask.

Do I have regrets at times? Sure, I do. But I don't beat myself up over them. What I do is keep my vow that I will not make that mistake again.

Whether your pain is self-inflicted, inflicted by others, or a combination of both, you can decide today to reframe it.

Your story will thank you for it.

Recap of Key Points:

- It's important to have a "What" and an emotionally compelling "Why" behind it.
- You can't help yourself by yourself—you need a "Who."
- Having a concise Story Line can inspire and focus your growth.
- It's important to take time to stop and reflect.
- One person it's important to forgive is yourself.
- Pain and challenges can benefit from reframing.

Reflection/Discussion Questions:

- Which item in the "Recap of Key Points" jumps out at you the most?
- Do you have an emotionally compelling "Why?" Why or why not?
- Do you have enough healthy people around you to serve as "Whos?" If not, how could you take steps to find one or two others?
- How hard is it to forgive yourself when you mess up? Why?
- What's a painful experience or challenge you've reframed?

MY STORY PLAN

What's your What? *(What is something you want to do or be?)*

What's your Why? *(What is your emotionally compelling reason?)*

Who's your Who? *(Who can you share your story with who can support and challenge you? What mentors have you sought out?)*

Whose Who are you? (see Chapter 7 for more on this)

What's your How?

- Do you really believe you can rewrite your story? Why?

- Your Story Line:

- Have you forgiven yourself, so that you are looking forward not backward?

- What's a pain/challenge you are reframing?

- What resulted from the conversations you have had about your story?

Choose your top two dragons to slay: (see Chapter 6 for descriptions of these)

- Busyness
- Over-comparison
- Perfectionism
- Blame
- Unforgiveness and bitterness
- Living someone else's story
- Setting unrealistic goals
- Expecting immediate results
- Over-listening to critics
- Lack of grace for my mistakes
- Shame

What's your plan to slay your top 2 dragons?

CHAPTER 6

THERE WILL BE
STORY DRAGONS

"It does not do to leave a live dragon out of your calculations, if you live near him."

- J.R.R. Tolkien

THE HERO'S JOURNEY

In classic literature, there's a pattern of storytelling called the "Hero's Journey." I'm sure several of your favorite books and movies borrow elements from it.

In the Hero's Journey, the adversary tries to prevent the hero from achieving a goal—Harry Potter had Lord Voldemort, Luke had Darth Vader, and in fairy tales, knights had to fight dragons.

While our real-life adversaries don't appear to be as dramatic as the ones facing our favorite literary or onscreen heroes, they can be just as debilitating. Your dragon may not breathe fire or be covered in scales, but it can definitely send you scurrying back to your castle, charred and unsuccessful.

In this section, we're going to explore the most common Third Story dragons. These fire-breathers can lumber out of their lairs anytime we approach the cusp of finally letting go of a distorted Second Story. Dragons prey on our fears and insecurities, and they are adept at finding weak spots in our armor. But by learning more about our adversaries, we can be better equipped when they rear their ugly heads.

Below are eleven of the most common dragons I've found, each with its own "Dragon Slayer."

1. BUSYNESS

We live in a day in which we measure our importance by our busyness. How many of us live our lives bouncing from one calendar event to the next? And how many of us feel weird or guilty when we find ourselves with nothing to do? Isn't that crazy?

Busyness is a formidable dragon because it cloaks itself in good intentions. Doing a lot and being a hard worker are admirable virtues. Doing too much? Not so admirable. What if the good things in your calendar are keeping you from great things? Writing and living in your Third Story takes time, and the dragon of busyness can be a constant distraction, sapping your time and energy.

> Dragon Slayer: Conduct a quick self-audit to examine how you're spending your time. Are you overspent? Schedule some time right now to work

on your Story Plan or just some time for you to do nothing! And set up a weekly calendar reminder for the next six weeks to pause and reflect on your plan and your progress.

2. OVER-COMPARISON

With the advent of social media, this dragon has grown larger than a jumbo jet. Every day, we're slammed with photos and stories of people who appear happier, richer, and more attractive than us. And many of these people are our friends!

When writing your Third Story, playing the comparison game sets you up to lose. You lose because your life isn't perfect, even though you know deep down that no one's life is. Dwelling on how you aren't as (fill in the blank) as someone else ends in a feedback loop of envy that is difficult to escape.

Even with your role models, it's easy to over-compare yourself to them and paralyze your progress on your Third Story. The most effective comparison you should make is this: compare where you were to where you are today.

> Dragon Slayer: Think of one of your traits you tend to over-compare and decide today to stop. Also think about your typical mindset as you scroll through various social media or other headlines—are you stealing the joy of your own journey by inviting envy or disappointment?

3. PERFECTIONISM

At first glance, the perfectionism dragon looks a lot like the over-comparison dragon. But there's a crucial difference. While comparison looks toward others, perfectionism looks inward. Perfectionists set unrealistic expectations of themselves, and then beat themselves up when they don't meet those expectations (did I mention the part about being unrealistic?).

There is nothing wrong with seeking excellence at home or at work, but perfectionism isn't the same as self-improvement. Perfectionism ramps up our desire to be better by attempting to perform at impossible levels. And perhaps most dangerously, perfectionism can set you down a path that will only lead to more guilt, anxiety, and self-judgment.

> Dragon Slayer: Quit setting unrealistic expectations for yourself and be okay with imperfections. Think about this question: How much of your guilt, stress, and pressure is related to you establishing perfection as your baseline?

4. BLAME

Like myself, I know many of you have come from difficult upbringings. When we experience hardships early in life imposed by other people, there are ripple effects. One of those ripples is blaming others from our past.

Blame is a type of dragon that curls up on your shoulder and tries to shift personal responsibility. When we fall into the habit of blaming others for our situation and our faults, we're ceding control of our Third Story back to those who wrote our

First Story. Blame is dangerous because it hands the pen back to other people.

I'm not suggesting your past is irrelevant. Far from it— it is important to process your past and any difficulties you experienced. You just can't stay there. Writing your Third Story isn't about blaming or being a victim, it's about confronting lies you've been told and the ones you've told yourself, and then finding freedom from those lies.

> Dragon Slayer: The next time you find yourself making excuses that shift responsibility of your narrative onto someone else, remind yourself— that's your First or Second Story talking. Who is someone you've blamed for some of your challenges? Now, shift your thinking back to something you do have control over, even if it's just your attitude or perspective.

5. UNFORGIVENESS AND BITTERNESS

I've encountered a number of people who have been difficult to forgive, and in most cases, they didn't deserve much forgiveness. But unforgiveness and bitterness root deep within our bones and only grow more toxic with age.

We stifle our story when we choose not to forgive. A Third Story fueled by bitterness isn't a story that leads to true flourishing. I love the quote by Lewis Smedes: "To forgive is to set a prisoner free and discover that the prisoner was you."

Forgiveness doesn't mean we minimize what someone did to us or that we become best friends with them. Forgiveness is about making peace with our past so we can move forward into our future. If we cannot forgive, a lens of bitterness blurs our writing.

Dragon Slayer: Digging through our First Story provides ample opportunity to generate bitterness, but we have a choice. We can't change the past, but we can choose to forgive. As you reflect, is any unforgiveness holding you back?

6. LIVING SOMEONE ELSE'S STORY

Many of us attempt to live out someone else's idea of what we should look like. How many times do we find ourselves living a version of ourselves that is really someone else's creation?

Living someone else's story plays into our desire to please the people around us—especially authority figures. "You shouldn't major in that subject…" or "I don't see you dating that person…" can feel less like suggestions and more like demands, or even threats. Maybe you're subtly—or not so subtly—being directed into someone else's dream for you.

I do want to caution you about this dragon—because it's also not wise to dismiss everyone's input just because it clashes with what you think your life should look like, so exercise judgment and wisdom when tackling this.

Dragon Slayer: Reflect on any family or friends who you might be attempting to live their story. Listen to their advice, but make sure any actions you take are a choice, not just a reflex to please others.

7. SETTING UNREALISTIC GOALS

I love when people have big dreams! Nothing makes me happier than watching people overcome their fears and open up to more possibilities in life. However, sometimes we set ourselves up for failure by establishing unrealistic goals and overblown expectations.

Have you ever run a marathon? I haven't—but I've driven one! I've heard that runners training for a marathon practice a mental strategy called "chunking" to get them through the arduous 26.2-mile race. Chunking is the art of breaking up the run into smaller sections. Instead of thinking, "I have to run 26.2 miles," they think, "I have to run five miles" (still sounds like a lot to me!), and once they pass the 5-mile marker they think, "I just have to run five more miles." By mentally breaking up the marathon into easier to manage chunks, the end goal appears more attainable.

If we immediately set out to tackle a huge goal, we can easily become discouraged when it is more difficult than we initially anticipated. When it comes to your Third Story, have big dreams but don't try to overhaul yourself.

> Dragon Slayer: Decide on a couple of very manageable goals and then use the momentum from accomplishing them to propel you forward. Think of a small habit you could be consistent with over time that could make a big difference. Ideally, even give yourself a fun incentive for reaching the incremental goals you choose.

8. EXPECTING IMMEDIATE RESULTS

Anyone who's tried to lose weight is intimately familiar with this dragon. Every January, the number of people purchasing gym memberships skyrockets as people set out to achieve their New Year's resolutions. But a few weeks later, gyms experience a predictable nosedive of interest as people realize that working out is hard work.

The same principle applies to our Third Story if we fall into the trap of "magical thinking." This happens when we believe there's a plan that's going to give us large, immediate returns. Most of the time, incremental work leads to incremental results, which is great!

Don't set yourself up for disappointment by deciding, "I'm going to be more confident" or "I'm going to strengthen a friendship" and then become thrown off when it doesn't happen overnight.

Change takes time, effort, and patience when writing your Third Story. It's a journey that will (quite literally) take your entire life. Let that be an encouragement, not a downer.

> Dragon Slayer: Think of a goal you have and focus more on your efforts toward the goal, not just on the final outcome. Do you have any goals that could set you up for disappointment because the timeline is too short?

9. OVER-LISTENING TO CRITICS

This one isn't just one dragon—it's a whole family of them—and maybe they're your actual family! If you write your Third Story, critics will come. And that's because it is so easy to be a critic. All you need is an opinion, and a mouth or keyboard.

Should you listen to feedback from others…even if it is poorly delivered? Yes. And yes. Listen, but then determine its value. There's a difference between someone challenging/stretching you and a critic who is just hurting you or trying to hold you back to make themselves feel superior. A good truth teller is someone who corrects and instructs out of a desire to see you be better. A critic is someone who just drags you down.

We need to make an important point in case you're thinking of a close family member or friend who is a critic and pondering, "Yeah, they do criticize me a lot. I should just cut them off!" Isolating yourself from them or putting up a wall may not be the best solution. It's possible you are too sensitive to criticism and that the critic is simply exposing that.

> Dragon Slayer: Is there a critic in your life who you give too much power? Do you ever set yourself up for disappointment by oversharing with them? Should you thicken your skin so when critics show up, you are less swayed by their remarks?

10. LACK OF GRACE FOR YOUR MISTAKES

As mentioned in Chapter 4, many of us are our harshest critics.

Sometimes we set out to write our Third Story, experience a setback, and then give up because we knew we shouldn't have tried to change or grow. Let me tell you something—that is a lie. And at no additional charge, I officially give you permission to mess up!

Writing your Third Story will not always be a road filled with rainbows and butterflies. Sometimes it will be difficult, and you may feel defeated. The most important (and difficult) lesson I've had to learn is to extend forgiveness to myself for periods of defeat. You are stronger than you know, and the reward is so much better than you can possibly imagine.

> Dragon Slayer: You don't have to wait on anyone else to change how you talk to yourself. Remember, you are only defeated when you dwell on negatives or mistakes. If you get knocked down, just brush off your armor, stand up, give yourself some grace, and get back into the fight.

11. SHAME

Shame is a universal human experience and emotion. It's a dragon that seems to appear everywhere. In her book *Daring Greatly*, Brené Brown defines shame as "the intensely painful feeling or experience of believing that we are flawed and therefore unworthy of love and belonging."

Humans are wired for connection. We aren't meant to experience our story alone. But shame erects barriers to human experience and tells us we don't deserve to participate. Shame is corrosive—it eats away at our self-image, relationships, and goals. It inhibits personal growth because it slyly (and convincingly) whispers in our ears that we aren't worthy.

When we write our Third Story, feelings of shame can feel inescapable. It's often not a matter of *if*, but *when* the dragon of shame will rear itself. So be prepared. Shame cuts deep, because it turns us against ourselves.

> Dragon Slayer: Know the difference between shame and guilt. Guilt says, "I *did* something

bad." Shame says, "I *am* bad." Be aware of environmental, relational, or verbal triggers that may generate shame. Also, shame dies in the light of truth and transparency—find a "Who" (or two) you can trust to discuss your feelings of unworthiness when they arise.

SELECT A DRAGON

On your Story Plan at the end of Chapter 5, pick your top two dragons that need slaying and add a brief plan on how to overcome them.

Recap of Key Points:

- Various dragons can impede us as we write our Third Story.
- It's important to focus on a dragon or two and have a plan to overcome them.

Reflection/Discussion Questions:

- What are your top 2 dragons that need slaying?
- Who could you share your top 2 dragons with?
- With your top 2 dragons, why are those a particular challenge?

CHAPTER 7

WHOSE WHO ARE YOU?

"Blessed is the influence of one true, loving human soul on another."

-George Eliot

INFLUENCE

You can't *not* communicate. My college speech professor taught me that. That means you're always sending messages, verbal or nonverbal. She was right, and life since then has convinced me of a related truth. You can't *not* influence.

We influence with more than just words. The looks we give our coworkers, the way we present ourselves in public, the micro-expressions that flit across faces—all broadcast messages that become etched onto other people's neurons and scribble on other people's stories.

That's great news, because you now know how to write good

stuff—encouragement, constructive feedback, support, and validation. You can point out reasons to celebrate and join—or even host—the party. You can confidently say, "You can do this," because you see qualities they may not see.

If you don't think you have influence, I have good news. That's just your First Story talking!

And what about if you've been writing on others and making an impact, but haven't been writing well? Maybe you have some regret for things you should have written more or some writings you wish you could erase. You can't just hit control-alt-delete, but you can at least start pressing the right keys now. You can own it and tell someone in your life, "What I've been meaning to say is…" or "Who I've been meaning to be for you is…"

It's never too late to start writing on others right.

Let's look at five ways you can be a "Who" for others and write on them:

1. The Power of Believing in Others
2. The Power of Traditions
3. The Power of Affirmation
4. The Power of Fun
5. The Power of Helping Others Reframe

1. USE THE POWER OF BELIEVING IN OTHERS

Monda Simmons didn't realize she was walking into what would become a dream job at South Houston High School—because it sure seemed like a nightmare. Teaching in a school where dozens of gang members roam the halls can blur your vision.

When her husband accepted the pastorate of a Houston church, she willingly resigned her position as chief information officer in a large Florida school district. It was a perfect chance to return to her first love, the classroom.

"I'm good to teach freshman English, history, or social studies," she told the principal.

A bit puzzled as he reviewed her impressive credentials, he replied, "This doesn't look like the normal résumé qualifications for teaching those classes."

With her unique background, her principal thought she might be a perfect candidate to champion a new classroom process called *Capturing Kids' Hearts.* She laughs now when she recalls that she had no interest first time he inquired. She wasn't interested the next time he brought it up, either.

But the third time he told her he wanted her to attend a *Capturing Kids' Hearts* workshop, he added, "And just to be sure you go, I'll drive our group."

By the end of the workshop, Monda was urging the principal to drive her back to Houston faster so she could start sharing the strategies she had discovered with their students and teachers.

The following semester, Monda taught two of the *LeadWorthy* classes that stem from *Capturing Kids' Hearts.* She admitted some jitters on the first day of class. "My eyes got big when I saw one senior's name on the roster," she remembered. "He had been in so much trouble, both in and out of school. His reputation involved drugs, violence, gangs, arrests, and incarcerations. I wasn't sure the program could survive him."

Monda greeted him that day with a handshake and full eye contact. "Hello, young man, my name is Monda Simmons," she said. "And you are?"

The senior reached out his hand and instead of replying with the gang nickname he typically insisted on, simply stated, "My name is Stanley Leone."

"Stanley, it's very nice to meet you," she said.

Stanley was taken aback. He knew she was aware of his reputation, but she was offering him something beyond her sincerity and sparkling eyes—a new start.

As the semester progressed, Monda saw leadership potential in Stanley. She voiced how much she believed in him, even when he didn't believe in himself. "Beneath your anger, I see a champion." She daily affirmed him with messages such as, "I believe in you," "You're going to be great," and "You're going to do something great."

On one especially rough day for Stanley, he responded flatly, "I don't think I'm great."

"I didn't say you *were* great—I said you *will be* great," Monda clarified. "You aren't great right now, so you need to make better choices and then you'll do something great."

Tears began to flow from Stanley and then from Monda, too. In Stanley's words, "She saw what I'd been hiding all those years."

Their class was a melting pot of life situations—freshmen, seniors, athletes, band members, popular kids, troublemakers—and of all ethnicities. Stanley later told Monda, "You helped us see that although different on the outside, we had one thing in common: we all understood pain."

As part of *LeadWorthy,* Monda facilitated the students in writing a Social Contract that became the glue for each class, helping build trust between students and with the teacher. They opened up to each other in their student speeches, many realizing for the first time that there were other people going through similarly difficult situations and they weren't alone. The students developed relationships with each other, building support and a sense of belonging.

One highlight of the semester occurred when Monda invited Stanley to speak to a group of teachers in Round Top, Texas. It touched Stanley to be surrounded by so many adults who made him feel important and wanted to hear from him.

As he shared his difficult First Story, emotions ran high for all in the room. Stanley said, "It was the first time I had an opportunity to vent. I struggled to finish telling my story that day through the sobs and tears, but sharing it with others allowed me to get it out and confront my emotions head on."

Monda's belief in Stanley eventually led to him receiving a college scholarship to Saint Xavier University in Chicago, and graduating magna cum laude. Today, he is an education strategist for the Flippen Group.

"Stanley became our firstborn son of the heart," Monda told me years later. "We never legally adopted him, but he calls us Mom and Dad. People talk about how I wrote on his life, but I'm here to tell you he wrote on mine too. In large letters."

Who is someone you can voice your belief in today?

2. USE THE POWER OF TRADITIONS

Traditions are cornerstones of a culture, consisting of events and activities that convince you and others that you belong. Effective traditions remind us we came from a good place and they put a stamp on our passport into a hopeful future.

Functionally, traditions tell stories, usually in an emotional and symbolic shorthand fully understood only by the participants.

Dr. Paul Zak's groundbreaking studies on oxytocin—what he terms "the moral molecule"—show that community bonding and mutual trust levels are positively impacted by all kinds of shared events, including (but not limited to) watching emotional videos, religious rituals, folk dances, weddings, and initiation ceremonies.

Who doesn't like telling stories around a campfire, bringing in the New Year with a kiss, or fireworks on July 4th? I have a granddaughter whose volleyball team is flooded with more traditions than I can count, with gobs of handshakes, chants, dances, and celebratory gestures! Traditions are all around us.

Let me share with you about what my Navajo friend, Shaun Martin, has accomplished with the help of traditions. He has been recognized at National Outstanding Rural Educator of the Year while being a teacher and cross country coach in Chinle, Arizona. His athletes have claimed 12 team state championships, 19 individual state titles, and 49 of his students attended college on scholarship. Shaun also champions the *Capturing Kids' Hearts* teacher training and *LeadWorthy* student curriculum.

In a video on YouTube (www.youtube.com/ watch?v=7QJp2lM9ShA), Shaun is dressed sharply with his long black pony tail behind him. With a bold, animated voice he asks a group of students sitting on a gym floor, "When the sun rises, what do the birds do? They chirp! They sing!" He continues, "What do flowers do when the sun rises? They open!" Lastly, he asks, "What do Navajo people do when the sun rises?" He lights up as he answers, "They run!"

No surprise that some of the biggest traditions in his life focus on joy and running. And as it should, joy comes first.

Navajo tradition puts great significance on an infant "receiving joy" with his or her first response to another person with a genuine laugh. This initial, from-the-heart giggle triggers a celebration. In that moment, the child takes the final steps to fully becoming human and joining the community. Of course, Shaun can't remember his celebration, but he grew up taking part when other infants received joy.

With some assistance at the celebration, this newest member of the community sprinkles rock salt on each person's plate and gives each guest a gift of joy. Imagine if you were taught, like

Shaun, that you receive joy when you first laugh, and from that time forward you have the power to bless others with happiness.

The second Navajo tradition coincided with his voice changing. Shaun literally ran to manhood.

For four days, he and other boys lived in an earthen lodge with a medicine man and were instructed in what they needed to know to be a man. But there was also serious physical application. Each morning the boys faced east and ran as far as they could. Every day they were expected to push themselves harder than the day before. On Shaun's last day, he not only covered more miles than the others—he ran further than anyone in memory.

That running tradition anchors his adult life. "Traditions connected me to my culture, so I knew I belonged," he says. "When life gets tough, I remind myself that what I did as a kid, I can do as an adult." He listens to the traditions as he runs, and wins, ultramarathons.

Luckily for the rest of us, traditions aren't just for Navajos.

As you reinforce meaningful traditions from your past, think about starting more of your own, such as:

- Big Words for Dinner: Every night each of our sons knew they would have to share a new word and use it in a sentence during the meal. One evening they staged an intervention to force me to admit I suffer from abibliophobia. "You showed the classic symptoms in childhood and today you really manifest the condition in the bathroom." Which is how I learned that abibliophobia is the fear of not having something to read!

- When the boys were attending college close to home, we had family night on Thursdays. It was a running joke how protective we were of that time. If someone got an outside request for that night, the response was always,

"No, that's our family night." We didn't have a big agenda or clever bonding activities, we just spent consistent time together and created shared memories (like the time we all cut into our chicken dinner to find it was raw...or when one son thought it was a compliment to tell the person who cooked, "This macaroni and cheese is as good as Luby's Cafeteria!"

- Sharing "Good Things" is part of the *Capturing Kids' Hearts* process in schools across the world. Teachers start class by asking students to share a quick good thing in life. It can be school related or personal. Two or three minutes sharing positive happenings sets a great tone for the rest of the class.

- I know grandparents who take their grandchildren to a nice restaurant to celebrate birthdays—just the three of them. The child gets undivided attention, learns there is more to eat than fast food, and practices conversing with adults. Aunts and uncles can do the same with nieces and nephews.

- A teacher can finish each class with a student reading an inspirational quote from the "quote bowl."

- A friend has a breakfast-for-dinner night every week. Another friend has a pancake breakfast every Saturday. Another parent simply takes his kids to breakfast on weekends.

- A colleague always takes two pictures at important family events—the bonus picture being a "silly face" version.

What are your traditions? If you don't have some good ones, not to worry. Borrow, create, or recreate some you can use to write on others around you.

3. USE THE POWER OF AFFIRMATION

There is often an assumption that employees do what they're paid to do, friends do what friends are for, and family members who already know how you feel don't need extra encouragement.

If you think that way, you are missing out on the Power of Affirmation.

A 2005 Gallup poll found that giving praise has a significant impact on a company's bottom line and employee retention. Workers who received recognition for doing good work in the previous seven days improved productivity, and those who did not feel adequately recognized were three times more likely to say they would quit within the next 12 months.

If you conducted similar research among your family and friends, I'm convinced you'd see similar positives from affirmation in those relationships, too.

Superintendent of Camp Verde Unified School District, Danny Howe, accomplished the impossible through the power of affirmations. By impossible, I mean that district discipline referrals went from 279 per year to 150, and then to 77.

Danny put an emphasis on strengthening connections, sharing positives, building relational capacity, and students supporting each other and taking each other under their wings. The focus paid off.

He told me about one girl, Melinda, who had been bullied throughout her school years. "Melinda experienced the difference affirmations made and she wanted to pass it on. She gathered up her close friends and they all decided to make a difference, one kid at a time. I'll never forget hearing her ask a teacher for the names of students who were having a bad day or who needed 'pepping up.' With names in hand, Melinda put her army of affirmers into action with notes and high-fives and verbal pick-me-ups."

As you utilize the power of affirmation, here are Four Tips for Affirmations:

1. Find the time.
2. Be specific.
3. Take it deeper.
4. Use the element of surprise.

FIND THE TIME

A common objection I hear from people who are asked to give more compliments is that they "don't have time to nurture everybody."

In a recent workshop my co-author Chris challenged a self-admitted non-affirmer to compliment someone in the room. After an awkward pause, the participant managed to eke out an affirmation about a colleague's attire.

"That compliment took about three seconds," Chris noted before asking, "Does anybody know how many seconds there are in a day?" After waiting long enough for people to attempt some rudimentary math in their heads, the resident statistician did the math for them, "86,400."

So, you don't need to blow up your schedule and dedicate massive blocks of time to compliment others. If you affirm just four people a day at three seconds each, you still have 99.99% of your daily seconds left to check off everything else on your to-do list.

Maybe you could add, "It's just three seconds" as a recurring item on your calendar. Or make notes when you see something worth praising in meetings. Train your brain to praise the praiseworthy.

Certainly, there are other times when longer affirmation sessions occur. One of my greatest affirmers was Essie Webber. I met him because I needed a summer job to pay my way through college. One of the few "help wanted" positions I could find involved sewer lines. And it wasn't a management slot!

Essie had little formal education, was in his late fifties and had been in the department most of his life. He worked hard, said little, saw that things were done right, and cared about people. I loved him. And equally, he loved me.

Every day, Essie and I spent time together—often standing in raw sewage. During those times (when I had to remember not to scratch my nose), he would ask me about my family and foster my dreams. He taught me, pointed out what I did well, and made me feel important.

His affirmation ignored racial and economic boundaries. Different races did very little mingling during that time, as segregation was unfortunately still alive and well in East Texas. But Essie invited me to supper anyway. After dinner, I remember sitting on their porch with Mrs. Webber, enjoying ice cream, conversation, and the summer breeze. That remains as one of the best affirmations I've ever received. Being invited home by my boss meant the world to me.

Essie taught me that affirming and spending time with people is worth it. He also taught me how to work, and to make work meaningful and enjoyable. I learned there is dignity in work well done, no matter what the work is.

BE SPECIFIC

I learned this lesson the hard way when I and a couple of colleagues were consulting with a client in New York City. The first day of the two-day workshop went incredibly well. For most of it, I was proudly watching my team in action, particularly my co-author Chris.

The next day I was emphasizing to the client the importance of nurturing others, and I asked Chris, "How many compliments did I give you about how you did yesterday?" He hesitated awkwardly so I repeated the question, "Seriously, Chris, tell them—how many?" Finally, he said, "Zero, I think."

I was floored!

As soon as we had a break, I asked Chris what "Zero, I think" meant. "Well, you did voice a one-size-fits-all 'Great job team' at dinner," he answered.

"But I looked at you when I said it!" I countered as I humbly smiled. But I knew he was right. "Great job team" is nice for general consumption—but it wasn't a great Chris-specific compliment.

There is added value in being specific. The more the affirmation zooms in on a specific effort, the greater the impetus for the receiver to repeat the behavior.

TAKE IT DEEPER

Chris is also a master at identifying appropriate and needed validation opportunities. He spoke recently at a family camp and modeled for parents and counselors not just the importance of writing affirmatively, but how to do it.

Toward the end of the three-day camp, he told them about the book we were working on—the one you're reading now.

"Taylor," Chris said, turning to one of the counselors. "You have been an amazing counselor for my kids this weekend. I'd like to write on you that you're a memory creator. You facilitate experiences that are permanently seared in kids' minds. That is an amazing gift and you have used that gift well."

Unexpectedly, someone else jumped in and spoke up.

"The person I'd like to write on is Sarah," a parent said. "Sarah, you are a thermostat. You set the temperature in a positive way and you bring people up."

Another person said, "I'd like to write on Emma that you are a sparkler. When you talk to kids, your eyes light up, and that makes the kids light up." "I'd like to write on Jake," said another parent, "You have a power you don't fully realize yet. Your words and actions carry a lot of weight, and you've impacted many people this weekend, including me."

Chris didn't tell the people to use the "writing on" terminology. It just happened. There's a difference between saying, "One thing I like about you" and "I'd like to write on you." "Writing on" someone is deeper. It's stickier.

USE THE ELEMENT OF SURPRISE

Studies show that while all real compliments have value, the neurological worth seems to climb when they are unexpected. And the greater the element of surprise, the more effective the affirmation. If the compliment is just a routine pat on the back—even though it is appreciated—it lacks emotional punch.

A Little League ball player who's had a bad game or an office worker having a bad week are focused on their failures. And that might be briefly needed if they want to improve their performance. But when someone else remarks on something they did well in the midst of the failure, that's the surprise compliment I'm talking about.

Search harder for unexpected opportunities to verbalize how you appreciate others or what you see in them. Keep regularly thanking your staff or team for being professional, but also watch for opportunities to give unanticipated praise for efforts.

Toward the end of my senior year in college, one of my professors, Dr. Harold Clements, blindsided me after class by saying, "You need to go to graduate school." I thought surely he had mistaken me for my brother. But after the next class he said it again, clarifying he knew exactly who I was.

I was hanging on by a thread to keep my GPA high enough to sneak out of town with a bachelor's degree and he threw me a rope marked "master's." He kept insisting until I grabbed onto the rope. And his affirmations continued, instilling enough self-esteem in me that I actually showed up at graduate school…and stayed, and graduated.

I'm pretty sure I wasn't the only young adult he prodded. Writing on students was what he did. He probably didn't remember those conversations even a year later, but I did. And I still do, many years later.

Some other great affirmation ideas:

- In our *Capturing Kids' Hearts* workshops, we have an affirmation bag for each person with their name on it that people can drop notes in during the workshop. A lot of school classrooms have followed this example (the teacher just needs to ensure no child has an empty bag!).
- Echo affirmations. If someone compliments another person to you, find a way to share it. "Rico told me what a great job you did on that project!"

- After a project milestone or a challenging stretch, write compliments on small paper slips, insert them into balloons (with the person's name on the balloon), and scatter them around the office. Have each person pop their balloon and read the comment either to themselves or out loud.
- Create an affirmation wall of honor and have team members highlight positive attributes of each other.
- Make a bigger deal out of good service at a restaurant or store. Speak to a manager, email someone in headquarters, or leave a note that writes on them. Ever noticed a link to a feedback survey on your receipt? How many have you filled out?
- Think of someone you can call, text, or email some encouragement right now. Don't overthink it—a quick "I appreciate how you…" or "Just thinking about you" could go a long way. One of our staff did this and got back a text with a shocked-face emoji, asking "Did you have a near death experience or something?" That response indicated she didn't affirm people very often! Another staff member sent a two-line "I appreciate you" email and got back a "You made my month!" response.

4. USE THE POWER OF FUN

We work hard at our office—and we laugh a lot. Those two activities are not mutually exclusive.

In fact, they are mutually supportive in the office, classroom, and living room.

I've found that a lot of people turn off their sense of humor at the office. They tell me, "It's work, so I don't want to joke around." I'm not suggesting clowning around on the job or being flippant about responsibilities, but in most workplaces, it can be advantageous, disarming, and culture-building when you integrate some fun into your day-to-day conversations and make people smile.

The science says so, as well.

According to the Harvard Mahoney Neuroscience Institute, "Studies have shown that good, hearty laughter can relieve tension and stress; boost the immune system, by reducing stress hormones and increasing activity among immune cells and antibodies; and help reduce the risk of heart attack and stroke, by improving blood flow and blood vessel function."

And a Yale Medical School study states, "Laughter and humor can be a tonic for the brain, as well. Triggering the brain's emotional and reward centers spurs the release of dopamine, helping the brain to process emotional responses and enhancing our experience of pleasure; of serotonin, to buoy our mood; and of endorphins, to regulate our pain and stress."

Immediately changing personas at work is tough. I often suggest people start at home with kids or grandkids and give themselves permission to be fun and silly. In so many ways, kids show us how to enjoy the moment without fretting about our image.

Our grandkids are so used to me playing that they just assume I'm game for anything. A few months back, I was reading the newspaper while a couple of granddaughters put various hats, jewelry and makeup on me and (I thought) tickled my feet. When I finally noticed what they were doing, my toenails were sparkly pink. I spent significant time the following day vigorously removing their artwork. Not that I didn't appreciate it, but it looked like I was bleeding! Of course, it was worth every bit of the hassle.

Chris, who is an organized, neat, planned-out guy, has applied this on the personal front, too. One day I heard his family van rumbling down the gravel driveway, and I walked out to greet everyone with a big smile. The van door slid open and my eyes got bigger than my smile. There was mud all over the floor and all over the people inside! It seemed that on the way over they had passed a construction site, vacant except for a "really cool" mud hole. Chris and his kids stopped and jumped in—clothes and all. Judging by the supersized smiles beaming from beneath the grime, those kids will never forget that outing. I waved off the offer for hugs, but I did take pictures!

The more fun we have, the stronger connections and relational capacity we build, and the safer we feel. Laughter sears in emotions and memories. People remember how we make them feel. And all of this makes people easier to write on.

Just remember one size doesn't fit all when it comes to fun. One family's mud frolic is another's king-sized yuck, and don't expect your shy relative to willingly sing karaoke.

A lot of highly successful companies have taken some fun steps by building in spaces to give employees fun breaks away from their desks. I know of a top ad agency in Dallas, Texas, with a room full of treadmills and ping-pong tables, adjacent to a half-court basketball floor that can be used for a 3-on-3 tournament or a yoga session. Of course, the owners ride their motorcycles to work and park them beside the basketball court, so it all makes sense, doesn't it? The verdict is still out as to the bottom-line effect of all this, but the message is simple: enjoy your colleagues as much as possible.

Here are some other examples of fun to increase serotonin in those around you:

- My colleague Joy surprised her boys and husband one night by leaving the silverware off the table. Just glasses, bowls—and spaghetti. Since the boys liked dogs, that day eating supper meant "eating like a dog." It may sound gross to others, but years later her sons still talk about it with excitement. And they see a mom who empowers them to be fun and free.

- Have family fun nights and take turns choosing the activity. That means even the five-year-old gets control when it's her turn.
- Celebrate birthdays at work by putting festive balloons and cards on the person's desk. For extra credit, put balloons on the path to the office.
- Add humor to an upcoming presentation you are giving.
- One brilliant teacher we know pulls a joke of the day out of a bucket. Every Friday, a student gets to do the honors.
- Or use one principal's idea: he gives custom awards by using old trophies with new names taped over the old ones!

5. USE THE POWER OF HELPING OTHERS REFRAME

My colleague Meredith's three-year old daughter, Ella, did a bloody double-knee-plant on their driveway one autumn afternoon. "As her look of shock turned to tears," Meredith told me, her husband David scooped Ella up as Meredith joined him in collective comforting. They tried to distract Ella with songs and snacks while they cleaned the gravel from her knees.

Soon the sobbing ebbed a bit and Meredith said, "I know that hurt, but guess what?" With excitement in her voice, Meredith continued, "This means you get to have your very first *Frozen* band-aid!" The band-aid featured Ella's favorite character from the popular children's movie of the same name. The pain didn't stop, but the crying did. The pain had been acknowledged and then revalued as a special rite of passage. And her daughter had her first experience at reframing.

As we grow up, we can try to will ourselves to better reframe, but it's nice to have others help with the process when we face issues more sinister than skinned knees. Some people think this is sugar-coating and ignoring how the real world works. They might even advise, "Quit being such a Pollyanna and deal with it!"

Well, in my professional world, a "Pollyanna" is considered mildly schizophrenic since she denied reality. In fact, Pollyanna Syndrome is an official diagnostic option and the subject of scholarly papers on individuals who are "unrealistically optimistic." If you're not familiar with the classic movie of the same name, let me explain. Pollyanna is an orphaned girl being raised by her soul-dead aunt. She has a highly honed survival technique she calls "The Glad Game" that consists of searching through the debris of catastrophe for a glimmer of hope. Personally and professionally, I think Pollyanna got a bad rap.

I don't see her denying reality or rejecting the deep and true pain of her circumstances. In fact, she is fully aware of the blows hammering her. Rather, I see her doing great work finding legitimate reasons to celebrate the flickering flame of hope in the surrounding darkness. She learned to reframe and helped change an entire community by teaching them to do the same.

REFRAMING...AND MORE

Ivan. Nary. Maurice.

Morri Elliott knows he will carry those names to his grave, "not because they haunt me but because they inspire me." He met the teenagers in 2007, his first year at Sacramento Academic and Vocational Academy (SAVA), and they gave him an accelerated introduction to their world.

"Those kids knew it all, from homelessness to relatives being incarcerated to having family members murdered," he explains. "That's our student body. Of course, they all don't have such extreme stories, but they all have some. Even one night homeless and not knowing what is coming the next day is enough to terrify a child."

Every school day, Morri comes to work with a primary goal to create a place where students can feel safe, which lets them learn and gives them a route to good jobs and life stability. He writes positive things on them and helps them reframe their tough circumstances and experiences.

As principal, he reverse-engineered the multi-campus school to a graduation rate consistently over 75%. The nationally recognized system also fully utilizes both *Capturing Kids' Hearts* and *Teen Leadership/LeadWorthy*.

I smiled at his enthusiastic joy as he pointed out, "With the challenges our students face, the high percentage finishing with a degree is a win by itself. But what really fires me up is that our kids are building tiny houses for homeless vets, fixing cars, and catering food for 200-person events. I'm revved up about the opportunities our kids are going to get after they leave here."

He's talking about the kind of opportunities, rare in their environment, that seem normal for people like Morri who grew up "comfortable, in a stable family." He could have lived the good life dictated by his First Story, far away from the downside of Sacramento. But his Third Story called him elsewhere. It took him to Ivan and Nary and Maurice…and to Zach.

On May 16, 2016, 18-year-old Zach was walking the few blocks back to campus after lunch when someone drove by and shot him multiple times. "Instinctively, he headed for the school," Morri said. "Badly wounded, he ran until he couldn't run anymore, then walked until he couldn't walk anymore, and finally crawled the final yards until he collapsed."

Why? What compelled Zach to do everything, literally everything, in his power to get to *school*? Why not home, why not the police station or behind a car to shield himself? For Morri, the answer is simple, "School probably was the only place in his life where he felt safe."

The EMT teacher, school nurse and a few other staff were the first responders. The ambulance took him away unconscious as the police homicide unit started working the scene because it seemed obvious to them that he was going to die. Except he didn't.

Morri was at a conference in San Diego and was on a plane within an hour of getting the news. "Flying home was probably the longest hour and a half of my life, not having any communication with my team during the flight and not knowing all of the facts," he said. "I made it back while Zach was still in the operating room. Even after the first surgery the doctors said the probability of survival for Zach was very low."

"One bullet entered through his abdomen and pierced multiple organs," Morri explained. "His recovery was an absolute miracle."

Vice Principal Tara Jones piped up to continue the story, "Morri won't tell you the rest. He bought the family a bed." In typical Morri fashion, he downplayed his part. "Well, I didn't pay for it out of pocket," he explained, "I asked his dad what the family needed help with, and his only response was, 'We don't have a bed for him.' So, we set up a fundraising account."

Morri and Tara and the others didn't just buy Zach a bed. They wrote on him by financing his future with pieces of their own lives.

The morning of our conversation, Morri spotted Zach's

younger brother and sister playing ping-pong during break time. I wish you could have heard the joy in his voice when Morri told me, "Because of what we created for Zach—a safe place—every child in his family is at school at SAVA today."

Notice he said, "we've created" just like he said, "we bought a bed." He powerfully writes on his co-workers, too. Co-workers such as Tara. Unlike Morri, she understands the students' situations all too well.

"I'm here because I want to help these kids overcome and reframe the same kind of challenges I fought through," she said. "I lived and saw up close just about everything they battle—a lot of ugly, ugly stuff."

I couldn't resist interjecting and asking her, "What was your compelling moment? What made you look at your life, at the Second Story you were living, and then to challenge it, to reframe it, to determine to be more?"

She replied, "It was pretty simple, actually. One day a relative asked me, 'Why don't you go to college?' You need to understand the context here. No one in my family—and I have a huge family—had ever finished college and now one of them was suggesting I do it."

Fast forward through a bachelor's degree in English, a master's degree in education, stints working at the California State Legislature, and time serving in the United States Army, and you see the outcome of that family member writing on her as she stands in her own SAVA classroom of kids she empathizes with deeply.

It didn't take long for Morri to spot additional gifts and promote her. "I didn't want to become an administrator," she admitted. "I knew I was a great teacher and making a difference. But Morri and some others convinced me I could do that even more as vice principal."

"Morri wants all of us to be better every day—and he believes we can and will be," she told me. "I've worked with some great leaders, but his leadership style sets him apart. So I guess," she added, "my emotionally compelling reason to continue writing my Third Story is to keep gaining self-esteem, and help others do the same thing."

That mission is being accomplished, according to Morri. "Every time I see Tara, there are three or four students clustered near her desk to be loved on and inspired and hugged. Our students are here because they want to be here, because they believe they can learn things that will help them have a better life. Is there a better feeling in the world than that?"

In other words, Morri and Tara find their fulfillment in writing on others and helping those students reframe their First and Second Stories into healthier Third Stories. If only we could all do the same.

Some important DOs and DON'Ts in helping others reframe:

- DO be present and just listen sometimes: "I really appreciate you sharing..." "That sounds really hard," "Tell me more..."
- DO be encouraging and voice positives: "I'm proud of how you handled..." "I can see how you are stronger now..."
- DO ask great questions—some exploratory, some with a goal to make them reflect.
- DO help them process and label their emotions.
- DON'T think of all pain as the same—getting a B- on a test and losing a pet are very different.
- DON'T dismiss someone's pain, so avoid a "Just get over it!" attitude.
- DON'T tell them, "You should just be happy!"

LONG ROADS TO NYAMAKATE

No matter where you start, Nyamakate, Zimbabwe is a long way from anywhere. The roads are dusty and the trails leading into the village are well-traveled foot paths.

Dr. Joe Emmert, my buddy since second grade, and I have seen a lot of the world together over the years. We've carried medical, dental, and school supplies to remote areas, plodding this time through Africa. We spent hours driving and hiking until we saw the small stone sign that pointed us in the right direction.

We approached a one-room school: broken-out windows, a compacted dirt floor, iron bars over the door, a huge piece of slate for a chalkboard, and desks that had certainly seen better days.

A teenage boy emerged and introduced himself. "I am Washington," he said in crisp British English. "I was named after the first president of the United States."

Admiring his sharp blue sport coat with gold piping around the edges, I asked if he always dressed so nicely. "Of course, sir," he responded, "I am the head boy, which means that I am the top student."

He sent another student to bring the teacher from his home— about 200 yards from the school. As we stepped inside, we met a group of five 15-year-old boys sitting in the corner and working on a math problem that was nothing but gibberish to me.

The teacher arrived with a wide smile and huge presence. "Ah, you must be lost," were his first words to me. "You're a white man and this is Nyamakate, Zimbabwe!"

We both laughed as I insisted, "I'm not lost. I just don't know exactly where I am right now!"

His smile was contagious, and he laughed a laugh that is

always a little bit louder—and longer—than expected, but you can't help but be swept into the joy of it.

He turned and walked over to his boys and gestured toward them. "We have had corruption in our leaders here," he explained about Zimbabwe, "But some day these boys will lead our country and that will change. I am building the future of Zimbabwe and they will lead it. When these boys lead this country, I will be happy when they do."

I was spellbound as he patted one boy on the shoulder and said, "They are the future. Can you see it?" I couldn't tell if he was asking me or them. The boys beamed at his proclamation and I stood there in quiet admiration of a man who had learned to write great and powerful things into the stories of the boys that sat in front of him. And he was writing deeply into their souls.

Then we turned our attention back to the math problem they were trying to figure out. I had never seen a math problem so complex—I mentally checked out as soon as someone said the word vector! He smiled again and said, "I love teaching math to them. Yes, this is a very good problem for them to solve."

At that point, he placed his hand on the top of another boy's head, shook it gently and jokingly and said, "The answer is in here, and my job is to get the answer out." Again, the laughter only a good teacher can bring.

I later asked him if the boys knew how difficult the problem was that they were working on and his response was perfect, "No, of course not. If they knew that it was so hard, they might feel they couldn't do it. They will get the answer, but it will take time."

I was sold. Those boys in Zimbabwe will solve that problem because their teacher believes they will. One of the most incredible things I walked away with that day was this question: How could

I walk into a school in the middle of nowhere and find this most amazing teacher who was writing the future of a country?

Later, he took me to see an engineering problem that his class had solved before I arrived—the problem of bringing water up from a well that is too deep for most hand pumps to work. His students provided a solution so that the villagers didn't have to walk to the river for water. As he told me this story, his face lit up and that beautiful laugh came out once again.

"That's a great story, but I thought you told me you were teaching math to them," I challenged him as we prepared to leave.

Confused by my statement he paused before clarifying, "Yes, I am their math teacher. I love teaching math to them."

"Actually, my friend, you are teaching them how to write," I said. "And to write on a large canvas."

Recap of Key Points:

- We don't fully realize our influence.
- It's never too late to start writing on others right.
- Traditions and ceremonies are a great way to write on people.
- Words of affirmation are powerful.
- Fun and a sense of humor help build healthy environments.
- An important skill to teach others is how to reframe.

Reflection/Discussion Questions:

- Which item in the "Recap of Key Points" jumps out at you the most?
- What would happen if you fully realized your influence?
- Think of someone whose milestone or incremental accomplishment you could further celebrate. What could you do and when could you schedule it?
- Who is someone close to you that you haven't complimented lately? Text or email them now.
- What's a tradition growing up that you enjoyed? What's a tradition you could start and/or better maintain?
- What's something fun you could do in the next week to write on others?
- How well are you reframing in your own life so you can better teach others to reframe?

CHAPTER 8

CONCLUSION

"Your time is limited, so don't waste it living someone else's life."

- Steve Jobs

WHAT IF NO ONE TAUGHT YOU HOW TO WRITE?

My wife, Susan, is the CEO of our company. I wanted her to join even sooner than she did, but I couldn't afford her at first—and yes, that means she is my boss! Who wouldn't listen to a brilliant wife and colleague who knows more than you do? Along with being an astute businesswoman, Susan is also the heart and soul of both our family and corporate culture.

She excels despite a childhood of dysfunction and instability, including separation from siblings and attending four different schools in 8th grade alone.

Some of her favorite people, those who wrote the positives on her, were her teachers. "They were there for me every day. They were a large part of my stability."

But like all of us, this articulate, strong, and accomplished woman still has some First Story scripts that linger in the background.

One evening, as we discussed her upbringing, she shared an experience I had not heard.

"When I was 14, if I couldn't buy my own food I just went hungry, so I took a job at Tastee-Freez, a fast-food and ice cream restaurant. One of the most challenging parts of my job had nothing to do with work. It was after work, having to walk back to the foster home alone late at night."

"I wish I had known you then," I said as I put my arms around her. "I would have walked you home every night." We both cried.

Nothing can change the brutal facts of her youth. But this particular script has been reframed emotionally. Those dragons were declawed by the affirmation of her as a beloved wife, mother, friend, and successful business leader.

I couldn't write on Susan during her First Story, but I can be part of her Third Story now. And in spite of—and maybe because of—the wounds she experienced, she excels at writing positively on others. It's clear how much she has written on me, and she has over 20 grandkids she writes on, too. Like in my story in Chapter 1, she would never be *here* if she hadn't been *there*.

If no one wrote on you well or taught you how to write, you can choose to use that void and pain to propel you. You definitely learned what not to do! Ask yourself—is your First Story a rock holding you down, or will it be a stepping stone?

LOOKING AHEAD

Many years ago, I dreamed about a ranch for kids who didn't have a loving family or safe home. It was on 500 acres, at the end of a road, laid out in a square, with pastures and creeks. But it didn't exist yet...or did it? Only a few years later, we put down $50 earnest money on a 499.97-acre ranch. That ranch opened and still operates today.

That was a dream of mine and I have more of them. But the question is, what are you dreams?

Life is a lot like driving in a car at night. You can only see as far as the headlights allow and then the view dims. But the illuminated part you can see is enough to get you where you are going. There are always twists, turns, hazards, potholes and unknowns, but that is also what keeps our attention on the road and makes the drive interesting.

You can't know all your future holds, and you can't write your full story today. And don't the best stories have sequels anyway?

Your Third Story is in your hands and the door to writing it is in front of you. Will you choose to walk through it? Will you quit believing lies about yourself and stop letting others make your life smaller than it could be? Since you didn't write your First Story, then why do you continue to live it? Why do you let it define and dictate your life?

Go ahead, write large and see what happens. Write with love and grace and goodness.

Write well—there are readers eager to see who you are!

You are more than you have yet imagined.

Write on, dear friend.

ABOUT THE AUTHORS

ABOUT FLIP FLIPPEN

Flip Flippen is the lead author of the *New York Times* best seller *The Flip Side: Break Free of the Behaviors That Hold You Back* and founder of The Flippen Group, one of the fastest-growing educator training, corporate talent, and team development companies in the United States.

Recognized as one of the top leadership thought leaders in America, Flip presents keynote speeches and leadership development events worldwide. Through a combination of powerful storytelling and psychological insight, Flip has introduced thousands of people to his process of identifying and eliminating the personal constraints that hinder growth and performance.

Flip earned a bachelor's degree from Stephen F. Austin State University and a master's degree from Texas A&M University. He invested the first 16 years of his professional life as a psychotherapist, opening a free outpatient clinic for at-risk youth and building a 500-acre residential treatment facility for boys in Central Texas.

Since founding The Flippen Group in 1990, Flip has led the company through development of breakthrough educational curricula and processes that are used in thousands of schools nationwide. Additionally, the company's business division works with Fortune 500 companies and multinational corporations, while the sports division works in talent development and selection for some of the most recognized professional, Olympic, and college teams in the world.

Flip has also contributed to hundreds of publications, including *Inc.* magazine and *SUCCESS* magazine, and has made appearances on the *TODAY* show, the *Super Bowl Pre-Game*, and Speed Channel's *NBS 24/7*.

Flip and his wife Susan, who is CEO of The Flippen Group, were named Ernst & Young Entrepreneurs of the Year and live on their ranch in College Station, Texas. In their spare time, they have also helped raise over 20 children.

ABOUT DR. CHRIS J. WHITE

Chris White is the Chief Science Officer at The Flippen Group. With his analytical skills and care for people, he helps solve people puzzles. This was demonstrated when he played a lead role in the development of the *Flippen Profile*, a preeminent psychometric assessment that allows individuals and organizations to identify and address the often hidden behaviors that frustrate personal and team performance. He has also built other assessments that present actionable individual and team insights, along with diagnostics and algorithms to identify common conflict patterns.

In over 20 years at The Flippen Group, Dr. White has performed 10,000 coaching sessions, consulted with elite teams and athletes in every major sport (including the Dallas Cowboys and New York Yankees), as well as with Fortune 500 executives, military generals, and top educators. He has keynoted, trained and consulted worldwide.

This is the second book he has co-authored. The first, *The*

Flip Side: Break Free of the Behaviors That Hold You Back, was a *New York Times* best seller and was translated into nine languages.

Dr. White earned a bachelor's degree in mathematics from Baylor University before receiving a master's degree in economics and PhD in statistics from Texas A&M University.

Chris and his wife, Jennifer, reside in College Station, Texas with daughters Harper and Berkley and sons Hudson and Braxton. He enjoys time with his family, playing and coaching sports, being outdoors, community service, writing poetry, and inventing things.

Printed in the United States
By Bookmasters